BAD Austen

The Worst Stories Jane Never Wrote

Edited by PETER ARCHER and JENNIFER LAWLER

Aadamsmedia

Avon, Massachusetts

Published by
Adams Media, a division of F+W Media, Inc.
57 Littlefield Street, Avon, MA 02322. U.S.A.
www.adamsmedia.com

ISBN 10: 1-4405-1185-3
ISBN 13: 978-1-4405-1185-1
eISBN 10: 1-4405-2944-2
eISBN 13: 978-1-4405-2944-3

Printed in the United States of America.

10 9 8 7 6 5 4 3 2 1

Library of Congress Cataloging-in-Publication Data
is available from the publisher.

Contains material adapted and abridged from *101 Things You Didn't Know about Jane Austen: The Truth about the World's Most Intriguing Romantic Literary Heroine*, by Patrice Hannon, PhD, copyright © 2007 by F+W Media, Inc., ISBN 10: 1-59869-284-4, ISBN 13: 978-1-59869-284-6; and from *Pride and Prejudice: The Wild and Wanton Edition* by Annabella Bloom and Jane Austen, copyright © 2011 by F+W Media, Inc., ISBN 10: 1-4405-0660-4, ISBN 13: 978-1-4405-0660-4

The following stories are works of fiction. The portrayals of celebrities and other culturally iconic characters within several of the following stories are wholly the creation of their respective authors. The actions and events in these fictional portrayals are not intended to reflect the real life activities, actions, or opinions of the source figure in any way.

Many of the designations used by manufacturers and sellers to distinguish their product are claimed as trademarks. Where those designations appear in this book and Adams Media was aware of a trademark claim, the designations have been printed with initial capital letters.

All interior illustrations © Jupiterimages Corporation

*This book is available at quantity discounts for bulk purchases.
For information, please call 1-800-289-0963.*

DEDICATION

For all the Jane Austen fans who've ever
put a pen to paper—or even just thought about it.

ACKNOWLEDGMENTS

The editors would like to thank all of the writers who played along and submitted their entries to BadAusten.com in the hopes of getting chosen to appear in this book. We had more fun at work than we're supposed to as we sifted through these stories and shared our favorites.

We'd also like to thank our panel of judges, Patrice Hannon, Carrie Bebris, and Gregory Bergman, for their involvement in picking the winning entry!

Contents

INTRODUCTION

What Is Bad Austen?

One afternoon, during a session of "We should publish a book on . . . ," our editors came up with the answer: Jane Austen. Who doesn't love Jane Austen? But this had to be a special book. A book that hadn't been done before. A book that would appeal to a lot of readers. A book that, in fact, made fun of Jane Austen. (She's dead—she can't sue us.)

The thinking went thusly: "There is a Bad Hemingway contest. There is a Bad Faulkner contest. There's even a Bad Bulwer-Lytton contest! Why not a Bad Austen contest? Surely as bad as we can make Hemingway be, Austen can be made worse?"

And so it was born, the Bad Austen Writing Contest, in which entrants turned their hands to penning scenes of a "classic" Jane Austen novel that never actually existed. We solicited Austen parodies on a blog (*www.BadAusten.com*) and collected the best into this book.

What were the rules? They were simple:
- Sharpen your wit, let your imagination run wild, and write a scene (no longer than 800 words, please!).

- You are free to determine plot, characters, and setting.
- Our only requirement is that the style must parody Austen.

Of course, we did have some legal mumbo jumbo as well, but that was basically it.

We also gave some guidance about entering the contest:

To enter, write a 500- to 800-word scene that is a parody of Jane Austen's writing. Possible themes can include, but are not limited to: horror and the supernatural, sex, science fiction, fantasy, romance, and mystery. The scenes may use Austen's characters or original characters created by you or drawn from real life (e.g., celebrities, sports figures, politicians, etc.). The scenes can parody themes, language, or characters and may be drawn from any of Austen's novels.

We found that many people saw the word *sex* and immediately got to work. So we have been reading about sex for weeks now, and as editors are unusually celibate creatures, this has led to some whining among the staff, and also some—well, that's pure speculation, so never mind.

Once we had read every single entry (some of them several times, with the door closed), we picked the one story we felt represented the pinnacle of bad Austen writing. It is probably best if we don't go into detail regarding how this selection was accomplished; suffice it to say that the process involved some arm wrestling and a few heated words, but no long-term damage was sustained by any of the parties.

We also picked the runner-up entrants to be published in this book, though admittedly this was a less rough-and-tumble enterprise as they did not have to be ranked in any particular order (imagine the carnage if they had). All told, we've included more than fifty stories for your enjoyment.

We saw that writers had submitted stories that split neatly into three categories (editors like categories): Austen-era entries, present-day entries, and mashups involving vampires (and sundry other creatures). This suggested to us a tripartite structure to the book (editors like parts). Thus, you will find that Part 1 contains stories that take place in the nineteenth century, Part 2 contains stories that take place in the present day, and Part 3 contains mashups of Austen and other beloved story lines.

We hope you enjoy!

The Winning Entry

Our distinguished panel of judges selected the following story as the best of the best, or the worst of the bad, whichever. The lucky winner not only receives the glory of being selected as the winner but also gets some cold, hard cash. We know Austen would appreciate that.

⤳ The Real Housewives of Bath-erly Hills ⤳
STEPHANIE WARDROP

Kyle Richards might quarrel with her, but Camille Grammer could find no quarrel with herself.

In her own surgically lifted eyes, Camille always deserved the best treatment because she never put up with any other—from women, at least—though it was beyond her how a former child actress like Kyle could be so insolent in her wit to a woman of her character, age, and situation. But upon reflection, and after consulting with her makeup artist and three of her four nannies, she realized that only jealousy, that plague upon the feminine half of the populace, could explain Kyle's incivility, that and only a party could put relations to right, or at least educate Kyle in respectable decorum.

The first invitation went out to Lisa Vanderpump, well known for her wise management of a series of dining establishments in the spa towns of Cheltenham and Bath, as well as her equally wise semireplacement of her graying husband with a mini Pomeranian. (Ken Vanderpump was no cad, certainly, but saddling a good lady with such an unfortunate last name was almost unforgiveable.)

Upon hearing Camille's voice on the other end of the line, Lisa suppressed a shudder, then smiled as widely as the Botox would allow.

"What a lovely idea," she cooed as she waved away Cedric, her permanently shirtless permanent houseguest. "I am excessively diverted. But how has Kyle affronted you this time, darling?"

"I confess I cannot fix on the hour, or the spot, or the look, or the words, which laid the foundation. I was in the middle before I knew that I had begun," Camille sighed as she looked out the window past the gardens below. "But I do recall her saying something about people only 'tolerating' me because of my famous actor husband, Kelsey."

"Oh, Camille, darling, do not vex yourself over such a trifle!" Lisa cautioned with her usual good sense. "For what do we live but to make sport for our neighbors, and laugh at them in our turn?" She recognized, after all, that it was not fair to expect Camille to feel how very much she was Kyle's inferior in talent and all the elegancies of mind. The very want of equality, Lisa reasoned, might prevent Camille's perception of it.

"Precisely why I thought a little pool party would be most agreeable! I know the sight of myself in a bikini never fails to raise my spirits—as well as those of most of the men around me," she tittered behind her hand. "We'll just get the girls together for a few drinks, a few hands of whist, and perhaps you will play the pianoforte?"

"That is so thoughtful, Camille," Lisa approved as she attempted to wrestle a miniature sombrero onto the tiny and recalcitrant head of her dog.

"Well, Lisa, there is nothing I would not do for those who are really my friends. I have no notion of loving people by halves! It is not my nature." Camille sighed at her own munificence.

"Of course, dear. Cheers!"

Camille next dialed the number of Adrienne Maloof, the most exotic and accomplished of her friends, who broke from her kickboxing routine to accept the call, however reluctantly. While certainly one of the more amiable members of society, Adrienne well knew that Camille Grammer was the natural daughter of nobody knows whom, with no settled provision of her own—though she would soon be eligible for a 50 million dollar alimony settlement due to her famous husband's perfidy—and certainly had no respectable relations. Granted, she had a little beauty and a little accomplishment as an MTV dancer and featured player in a few soft-core porn productions, but these honors led most of Adrienne's set to view Camille with the disdain for the vulgar normally reserved for the Misses Kardashian.

"Oh, Camille," Adrienne said rather hesitatingly. "Are you quite certain this is the soundest of plans? Angry people are not always wise, you know." And Camille was, despite her affectless smile, one of the angriest people Adrienne knew. Surely this party would prove once more that vanity working on a weak head produces every sort of mischief.

Camille paused, sensing a polite and cowardly dodge in the offing. Obviously, even the incomparable Ms. Maloof was not immune to that most pernicious of female maladies.

"I have no wish to incommode you," Camille assured her, "but do come."

Before returning to the kickboxing ring—and breaking her husband's nose for a third time—Adrienne promised she would at least try to make the engagement, though privately she could foresee any number of fortuitous obstacles to this plan.

PART 1

The Books Jane Never Wrote

Of the many entries we received in the Bad Austen contest, a fair number of them were set in Austen's era, although we have our doubts as to whether events could have actually occurred as alleged in any of these stories. That reservation notwithstanding, here, for your amusement, are those stories set in Austen's time that we felt sure you would enjoy.

⌁ Farthingale Junction ⌁
FREYA SWANSON

Upon hearing the news, Miriam Cauldwell could scarcely believe that anyone could have mistaken Colonel Prickett for a pheasant. She could not think of two entities more dissimilar, and yet, someone within the hunting party had shot the Colonel dead upon his estate, Perfunctory Hall. The very idea that a man with so distinguished a military career could be killed by a neighbor who mistook him for a game bird was too abhorrent for words.

"And the boy to whom it is entailed? What of him?" Great Aunt Lavinia demanded of Mrs. Cauldwell, Miriam's mother and her only niece.

"The boy is a man; Colonel Prickett's second cousin, a Mr. Samuel Farthingale."

"Yes? Well, what of him?"

Miriam bemoaned the listing of Mr. Farthingale's vital statistics, which everyone seemed to keep repeating for her benefit. The day before the accident, a man from London named after a petticoat would have been fodder for every person in _____shire. Sudden ownership of Perfunctory Hall, however, made him the most handsome man in creation. Unfortunately for Miriam, twenty years of age and still unmarried, Lavinia appeared to see Mr. Farthingale as her last great hope.

"—and is a very successful businessman in his own right."

"What business is that, Mama?" Miriam asked, with no interest whatsoever in the answer.

"He imports cloth, dear," said Mrs. Cauldwell.

"Cloth? Mr. Farthingale imports cloth?" cried Miriam. She could not believe it; Mr. Petticoat imported petticoats?

"Ring the bell for tea, dear," said Mrs. Cauldwell in such a tone as to assure her there would be no sort of merriment concerning the Colonel's heir.

The first opportunity for society to see Mr. Farthingale was at the funeral. He was pronounced a dignified mourner, and all the more handsome for looking so well in black. He was polite, if a little distant, but that was to be expected after a loss in the family. Most everyone in the county believed he would be married by Christmas. When Epiphany passed without a whisper of engagement, necessary measures were taken. Great Aunt Lavinia, dowager Empress of _____shire, would hold a ball at Hammerstone.

Hammerstone was an imposing estate littered with medieval fortifications and the ghosts that supposedly haunted them and was therefore impossible to make inviting from the exterior. Upon entering, however, the foyer led to what everyone simply called "the junction." It was here that medieval masonry gave way to neoclassical columns, and Lavinia's well-appointed home truly began.

It was a glorious ball, but Miriam was the only person truly enjoying the evening, for the most important guest had been delayed in London and would either be very late indeed, or not appear at all. Having at least temporarily escaped being paraded about like chattel, Miriam danced, and laughed, and was inadvertently quite charming. Lavinia looked upon it as a terrible waste; what was the point of being witty and gorgeous in front of married men and dour clergy? In the course of the evening, it became apparent that Lavinia had taken several glasses beyond prudence, resulting in her telling the Right Reverend Cummings that, yes, absolutely, their Lord and Savior would greatly enjoy a good novel.

Did You Know?

Jane Austen was born at home in the Steventon parsonage, Hampshire, England, on December 16, 1775, the seventh child of the Reverend George Austen and his wife, Cassandra (née Leigh). One more child would follow Jane three and a half years later—a boy. Jane would then have six brothers and just one sister, the beloved Cassandra. The large family lived on a clergyman's small salary supplemented by earnings from the boys' school run by Mr. and Mrs. Austen. The rectory was also a working farm, with fields of crops, a dairy, and a poultry yard.

Miriam had greatly enjoyed that conversation and felt no remorse for quietly prodding her great-aunt further into the discussion at the time, for the Reverend was always a good sport and had a quick wit himself. After, however, it became clear there was no reining her in now she was begun, and poor Mr. Farthingale had thought it polite to put in an appearance, regardless of the lateness.

"Oh, huzzah! He is come! Miriam! Where are you, child? He is come!" Lavinia did not wait and made straight for her unsuspecting guest.

"Mr. Petticoat! We were afraid you would not come! How was London? Is your business complete? Of course, it is—here you are. And in such a lovely vest! You are a handsome devil, Mr. Petticoat! Where is Miriam? You come with me, sir, we will find her!"

By then she had hold of his sleeve and dragged him across the ballroom. Miriam slipped behind the musicians and made for the foyer before her overly enthusiastic great-aunt could embarrass the young man any further, but Lavinia spotted her and shouted across the room for all to hear, "Miriam! Stop at the junction! I'll bring him to you!"

Miriam could not respond, nor could she disobey, and dutifully waited, hiding behind a column.

"Come, sir, this way!" Lavinia shouted as, sleeve in hand, she dragged him back across the ballroom.

"Yes, um, perhaps I should greet the other guests?"

"Other guests, what? No, no, no, to the junction, my boy, Petticoat, junction!"

⌐ An Unexpected Guest ⌐
BRANDY HEINRICH

Elizabeth was quietly reading at the feet of her sister Jane, who was working on a dainty piece of embroidery. The sisters had been retired to the drawing room in companionable silence for most of the morning, each deep in thought, reflecting on the events of the previous evening at the ball in Meryton. Jane was fondly thinking about the charming Mr. Bingley, while Elizabeth's thoughts weren't quite so charitably inclined toward Mr. Darcy's detestable behavior toward her. Their twin reverie was broken by the excited shouts of younger sisters Lydia and Kitty, who bounded into the room accompanied by chants of "A visitor! We have a visitor!"

Kitty beamed and twirled her skirts while Lydia concentrated on fixing the satin ribbons in her hair. Jane, thinking that perhaps Mr. Bingley had come to call, quickly settled herself back on her settee in what she hoped was a beguiling pose. Mr. Bennet, roused from his study by his boisterous daughters, stalked into the room, trailed by his wife. Mrs. Bennet fussed at her younger daughters, prattling on unheeded about a Big Blue Box and a ridiculous cravat. "Really. I've never . . . so inelegant. And to come to call on a family of our society, dressed in such . . . untidy attire! What will the neighbors say?"

Elizabeth inquired after the whereabouts of their mysterious visitor, caught up in her sisters' infectious excitement. Mr. Bennet, having seated himself by the window and in the midst of lighting his pipe, gestured expansively. "Says he's a doctor. . . ." At which point, he was interrupted by his wife going on once again about blue boxes in the lane and nattily dressed gentlemen masquerading as country physicians, to which her daughters paid no mind. Lydia clapped her hands in childish excitement, exclaiming "La! A doctor!"

At that precise moment, the drawing room door opened, silencing all of the assembled Bennets. The man standing in the doorway adjusted his bow tie and cleared his throat. "Ah. Yes. I do apologize, but I've only just realized I've come at a bad time, and—" to which the girls politely demurred that it was, in fact, a perfectly reasonable time and, as social obligations dictated, bade him to sit with them. Mrs. Bennet quickly sent a crestfallen Kitty to arrange tea for their impromptu gathering.

The stranger, looking quizzically at an instrument resembling a flameless candle, explained, "Well, you see, I seem to have arrived a bit early. I should be here later in the narrative. Right about the time Miss Elizabeth Bennet realizes the nature of her true feelings for Mr. Darcy."

Did You Know?

Jane Austen's mother was very proud of her high connections. She was born Cassandra Leigh, and many of the Leighs had become nobility themselves or married into the aristocracy. Moreover, her uncle Theophilus Leigh held the esteemed position of master of Balliol College at Oxford University. Mrs. Austen was certainly clever enough herself to justify a suspicion that Jane's intellect was the greatest manifestation of a Leigh trait.

Elizabeth issued a shocked declaration of her intention of never having any kind of positive feelings toward such as man as Mr. Darcy. Mrs. Bennet took up her daughter's discarded book and proceeded to fan herself quite vigorously, having worked herself up to an almost apoplectic state at such an idea as her dear Lizzie and the arrogant and aloof—and very wealthy—Mr. Darcy.

Having made another unintended social faux pas, the stranger retreated from the room into the hall, where Mr. Bennet, who was also intent on making his escape, joined him. At that moment they were passed by Mary Bennet, so intently reading aloud from a well-used copy of Fordyce's *Sermons* that she did not seem to even see the oddly attired stranger and quite passed him by without even an acknowledgment.

Apologizing for his daughter's lack of manners, Mr. Bennet took his guest by the elbow. "Young man, now that you have sufficiently shocked and scandalized the women of my household, let us retire to the study so that you may tell me all about that marvelous contraption of yours. You say it has something to do with time. . . ."

⟶ Hubris and Humiliation ⟵
MARIA HOPE

"In vain have I struggled. It will not do. I must have you!"

The last thing in the world Elizabeth Bennet expected was to see Mr. Darcy walk into the parlor where she sat alone, having excused herself from dining at Rosings that evening. His proposal of marriage caused even greater surprise. Although she thought him a jackass whose sensitivity could fit neatly within one of the thimbles in the sewing basket she had laid aside as he entered, she listened with a calm demeanor. Only by reminding herself, "I am a gentlewoman. I am a gentlewoman," was she able to refrain from a display of anger at his unbridled audacity.

But his appalling proposal grew worse. She watched him in silent amazement, doubting her ears but eventually having to acknowledge she was hearing correctly. If the way to win a woman was to tell her that loving someone with a family like hers was a horror exceeded only by his expectation of the gnashing of the teeth and tearing of the hair this announcement would incite within his own family, then Mr. Darcy most certainly would have succeeded. Unfortunately for him, she was not the woman for whom this method of wooing would be successful.

Since she could see he truly had no idea of the true consequence he was wounding, she decided to find in his injury to her the means of retribution. She let him finish. Seeing his obvious assumption at his conclusion, that she was his for the asking, nearly made her lose it.

She endeavored to stay her course. Hoping this would be just enough poetry to kill whatever vague inclination he had for her, she turned her rejection into doggerel. "But, sir, you yourself own it true. I am certainly not good enough to be a wife for you."

Mr. Darcy, who was leaning against the mantelpiece with his eyes fixed on her face, seemed to catch her words with surprise, and then condescension.

"But, my dear—" he began, only to be interrupted by her quick interjection, "No, sir. Really, I cannot accept your proposal. I am not good enough."

"But you must. I insist!"

She drew a breath before offering her counterproposal. "Sir, have me you will, but not as your wife. Come to me tonight for the time of your life. My window faces the lane, and it will be open. Don't disappoint, climb up my trellis, I'm hopin'."

He heard with shock, disbelief plain upon his face, and—the reaction that eventually overwhelmed those feelings—keen interest. Wanting to assure that he understood correctly, he said, "You would take me to your bed? And you a maiden?"

"You have told me all the reasons you shouldn't marry me, and yet, you insist you must have me. Is this not a better solution?"

He changed colour before her eyes at the proposal. The man who spoke forcefully before, words flying from his mouth in arrogant haste, now seemed indecisive.

Seeing this, she seized the initiative with a subtle sweetness and gentleness of manner designed to lull him. "If my willingness to bed you without marriage provokes some change in your feelings, then it's probably exactly as you thought—that you liked me against your will and have now returned to reason. But we certainly both agree, I am a most unacceptable choice to be your bride."

Elizabeth hoped this would silence him forever. To her dismay, he replied with no little assumed tranquility, "I will come to you as you offer, and when I am finished, you will not be able to deny yourself my lifelong association."

He continued, following her earlier example in rhyming, "Once you have had the best, there is no returning to the rest. Once you have lain in my arms, no other will do. You will beg me to marry you."

Unable to help herself, Elizabeth felt her mouth drop open. The man did, indeed, exceed her expectations. She had thought she was angry previously, but now she found herself nearly biting through her tongue to hold back her words. When she felt she could speak calmly, she allowed herself only to say, "Tonight then," and quitted the room.

On her way to the bedroom where she had been sleeping while a guest at Hunsford Parsonage, Elizabeth smiled as she passed the bedroom whose directions she had given to Mr. Darcy.

Mr. Collins slept there alone most nights, except for Saturdays when his wife, Charlotte, visited before returning to her room. Since tonight was Friday, Elizabeth could know for certain that Mr. Collins would be alone to receive Mr. Darcy as he climbed into the window.

⌐ Absinthea Pillock's Charm School for Girls Whose Fathers Can Afford Tuition ⌐
MARGARET FISKE

On a brisk morning, late September in North Trollop Downs, the cold breath of autumn plucked the first tender leaves of summer from their branches. Once again, 'twas time for Orientation Day at Tartfield Academy.

A new crop of pigtails, fresh from the hedgerows, filed into the lecture hall in their crisp pinafores and settled on the polished oak benches with their slates poised to record the lessons that would ensure their matrimony to suitable husbands.

As a rather striking woman clad in plum took the podium, the clank of heavy chains could be heard securing the exits. "Welcome to Tartfield, ladies. I am your head mistress, Absinthea Pillock."

"Good morning, Mrs. Pillock," chimed the pupils.

The head mistress slammed her merry-widowed fist on the lectern with a clamorous ferocity. "Nay! You shall address me properly as Miss or Mistress, never Missus. Nor should you assume that you shall become wifely candidates based solely upon the fact that your fathers produced the tuition to enroll you here.

"The grim facts are threefold: Firstly, many women will never march the chapel aisle. Secondly, those who do wed often find their husbands unsupportive and must sustain the household by their own means. Thirdly, the world is full of widow makers galore.

"While most finishing programs produce graduates full of fraudulent hope for an impossible future, Tartfield faculty foster no such false expectations. Traditional schooling makes girls far too clever for the pastoral oafs of the township, yet still beneath the affections of gentry."

The girls squirmed nervously in their seats.

"When do we begin pianoforte, and the embroidery of silk ribbons, and china painting?" asked Alice Singletwit.

"Never," replied Absinthea. "Such frippery earns you an early, unmarked grave in Potter's Field. However, if you merely remove that paintbrush from the undecorated china plate and rub it elsewhere, you will achieve happier results, Missy."

Prim Jenny Periwinkle's lower lip trembled anxiously. "What exactly are we to learn here?"

Mistress Pillock continued with a rejuvenated vigor. "We teach real-world skills for survival in a manless domicile. First-semester curriculum presents Introduction to Gutter Sniping, Recognition of Items One Cannot Afford, How to Nurture Multiple Cats as Substitute Kin, and tutorials on Cottage Maintenance for Dunces.

"Second session expands on these themes with informative lectures about Staving Off the Scythe of Death by Resale of Other People's Rubbish, Embracing Your Inner Crone, and Cuisine Derived from Things You Can Catch (which features the preparation of hearty dishes such as Rodent Étouffée and Mayfly Surprise Casserole). Also, we cover Ways Not to Waste One's Primary Childbearing Years Governing Other People's Offspring for a Pittance.

"Trimester courses focus on the corporal delights and development of one's Sza Sza Szu. You will leave here with the scruples of a barn cat, eager to strut the cobblestones for profit. Highlights are to include Working the Maypole 101, Overcoming One's Gag Reflex, and Advanced Mistressing."

"My father shan't like these topics," said Eliza Frost frigidly.

Absinthea tittered. "Poppycock! Your father had the prudence to send you to our academy. He understands that many a gentleman prefers a bit of tartar sauce on their cod, a little something-something that may be absent on the wife's home menu. So, tart you up, we shall. Here, you will be kept abreast of the latest methodology for snaring a weaker woman's spouse. Here, you will master the art of trapping a bachelor at the altar by the fabrication of hysterical pregnancy or other vile trickery.

"Today, we shall finish with a preview of the Classical Male Anatomy Laboratory, which offers scholars a rare opportunity for hands-on experience."

Although most of the audience was gingerly weeping, Miss Pillock did not cease.

"Observe," she said, thrusting a lever. A curtain dropped, exposing Custodian Dobbins in a state of jubilation, sporting only a grin and a hickory pointer. Little Mary Goodhead swooned and fell into the aisle, splayed in a most salaciously undignified fashion.

"Marvelous!" said the head mistress. "You're catching on already."

Did You Know?

Girls' schools make several appearances in Austen's novels, and Austen never has much good to say about them as institutions of learning, although she shows sympathy for the women who work in them. Mrs. Goddard, who runs the boarding school Harriet

Smith attends in *Emma*, treats her boarders with great kindness, but she cannot be doing much for their minds. A much harsher reference to such places appears in the fragment of a novel Austen began that we know as *The Watsons*. Emma Watson protests that she "would rather be a teacher at a school (and I can think of nothing worse) than marry a man I did not like." Her sister Elizabeth replies, "I would rather do anything than be a teacher at a school. . . . *I* have been at school, Emma, and know what a life they lead; *you* never have." This exchange also certainly shows that many women were faced with nothing but bad options when it came to figuring out how to provide for themselves in life.

⌒ The Horrors of Expectation ⌒
Matthew P. Mayo

Lord Dalnabbie paused, his hand trembling above the drawing-room door's brass handle. Would she think him too forward? Too brazen? Would she deign to glance his way at all? Oh, he hoped not. Not on this day, no, no, certainly not today. Or tomorrow, for that matter. Oh dear, what if she greeted him with a "Good morning, m'lord." How does one answer such an offering? Day after day, always the same. It was all too much.

On the other side of the drawing-room door, Tilda, the housemaid, tidied the young mistresses' sewing basket—the girls were such flibbertigibbets. Much like their mother, Lady Dalnabbie, who lamented daily of ever finding them suitable husbands. And daily, Tilda quelled the urge to shout that the little demons would be lucky creatures indeed to end up wedded. Given the odds, she prayed for their betrothal. Tilda did not look forward to spending her future years doting on the two Dalnabbie dimwits as they fluttered into spinsterhood.

Now, Lord Dalnabbie, he was a different sort. Tilda wondered how he had ever managed to marry. Peculiarity rode him hard, as Bonn, the stable boy, said. Indeed, Tilda had spied the master alone many times in the library, smoothing his vest front, sitting stiff and straight, an unopened book beside him on the sofa. He would glance about, a half smile twitching on his mouth, seeming forever on the verge of apologizing for causing possible offense to himself.

Lord Dalnabbie bit down on a tight knuckle. This would not do. He withdrew his hand from its near grasp of the brass door handle. No, not this way. With a quick, bold gesture, surprising even himself, Dalnabbie stuffed the trailing end of his handkerchief into his cuff, but could not keep from staring at the door. He fancied he almost heard the soft sounds of Tilda neatening the room. Tilda. His breath paused, and with a sudden willfulness summoned from his very slippers, he turned in the hallway of his ancestral home and remounted the stairs. This would not do at all. . . .

Inside the drawing room, Tilda heard the master dithering. She narrowed her eyes and considered racing for the door, recalling that morning years before when she had opened it to find him standing there. She had shrieked, then apologized and curtsied low. But his paroxysms had lasted for days. MacNee, the valet, had told her that, buried under layers of bedding, Lord Dalnabbie had twitched and wept as if he bore the world's shame on his shoulders.

And yet, since his recovery, she knew that he descended the stairs each morning, hovering in the passage outside the drawing room, like the shadow of a ghost, trembling, reaching, but never quite grasping . . .

Good heavens, thought Tilda as she tied back the last curtain. It's his house, after all. Bonn was right—money is wasted on the rich.

Upon reaching the top of the stairs, Lord Dalnabbie paused, one foot poised above the final step. Though he knew it to be carpet, and thus suitable to disguise his footfalls, he suspected that his timing this morning had been off. He had, of course, read about such things happening to perfect strangers in faraway places, but to date it had not happened to him.

He set down a tentative left foot, to act as a guide. Then, and no doubt urged forth by the very keeper of the gates of hell himself, first one, then both of the girls' bedchamber doors wrenched inward as if forced by storm gales, and his daughters, dressed for the morning, thundered toward him, hooting like gibbons.

Tilda paused at the bottom of the stairs on her way to give Cook a hand. She heard the girls' doors, their feet on the upper landing, their shouts. *And so begins another day*, she thought, looking up at them, her teeth tight behind a smile.

At that precise moment, Dalnabbie glanced downward, toward the bottom of the stairs, the very direction from which he had just returned. There stood Tilda, who had appeared as if from nowhere at all. There seemed no escape. Assault from below and from above. He glanced again. Yes, he was certain of it. No escape.

Lord Dalnabbie felt his mouth move, trying to form words. With all of their mother's grace, his daughters pushed by him, braying and stomping down the stairs. Toward Tilda, dear Tilda . . .

Dalnabbie trembled as if he were a leaf in a gale. He could not move from the top stair, even as a new horror swept over him—soon his wife would rise. Soon, and she would expect a response to her greeting. Oh, it was all too much. . . .

⌒ Proper Order ⌒
MICHAEL WRIGHT

Lady Catherine opened the small leather-bound volume and read, *It is a truth universally acknowledged that a single man in possession of a good fortune must be in want of a wife.*

"Poppycock," said Lady Catherine. In her youth she had known many wealthy unmarried men whose only interests were to slaughter large quantities of game birds and to consume even larger quantities of intoxicating liquors. She closed the book and reached for a volume of Fordyce's *Sermons.*

The following Tuesday, when her niece made her weekly visit, Lady Catherine inclined her head in the direction of the morning-room table. "You may retrieve the novel you so kindly brought for me. I found it quite stupid."

"Why, Aunt, you did not enjoy the story?"

"My dear Jane, I did not attempt to read the story, after encountering the absurd premise given in the first line."

"But, Aunt, it is a most delightful tale of obstacles overcome on the way to achieving happiness in marriage."

"In that case, I am glad I did not continue reading. It is my firm belief that literature should seek to uphold the virtues of an ordered society, not indulge the wanton emotions of parlor maids. Happiness in marriage, indeed!"

"I assure you, Aunt, that the books of this author serve not only to entertain but to instruct. Perhaps you might enjoy another of her works."

"*Her* works? The author is a woman?"

"A lady, Aunt, as is indicated on the title page."

"An error, no doubt, of the printer. A lady does not compose works of fiction."

"No doubt it is as you say, Aunt. But the books are nevertheless edifying."

"Give me an example of what you presume to be an edifying lesson."

"Here is another novel, in which a young woman of good family is persuaded to deny her suitor because he is poor."

"The proper course of action, indeed."

"That is not the outcome, however. The suitor acquires glory and fortune in the navy, returns after ten years to woo his first love, and convinces her to marry him."

"Absurd. Mature men should, and do, marry girls of child-bearing age, to ensure healthy offspring. It is apparent that the author has no experience of actual life."

Jane appeared to sink in her chair. Lady Catherine lightly touched the back of her niece's hand. "Don't take on so, Jane. When you are married and have acquired some experience of the world, I'm sure you will concur in my opinion. And sit up straight, my dear; good posture is the foundation of a good life."

"I understand, Aunt, for you have told me oftimes, that I require the firm influence of a husband to mold my taste and understanding, and I look forward eagerly to undergoing such edification. To that end, perhaps I might interest you in another of the author's works. It tells the story of a giddy young girl named Emma who is gently instructed in proper behavior by an upstanding friend of the family. In her gratitude, and with full understanding of the man's virtues, she marries him."

"Now that," replied Lady Catherine, with a sharp nod, "appears to be a sound tale. How are the moral lessons portrayed?"

"Most amusingly," said her niece, sitting up in her chair. "The young heroine attempts to arrange a marriage for her friend, with disastrous consequences. The hero shows her the errors of her schemes."

"Quite right. An unmarried woman should not attempt to settle such affairs on her own. Once she is married, however, such activity is rightly within her purview."

"And then," said Jane, "she speaks sharply to a poor and garrulous woman in the village and is rebuked by the hero for her behavior."

"Quite ridiculous. A gentlewoman is privileged to speak as she pleases to the poorer classes, without the interference of anyone, man or woman. I cannot countenance any further discussion of this 'lady' author." Lady Catherine rang for tea. "I trust that you will refrain in the future from reading fiction with such subversive intent. Please take this copy of Fordyce's *Sermons*, wherein you will learn the proper ordering of society."

⌒ Insult and Insolence ⌒
JACLYN LURKER

In an effort to protect his ancestral estate, Thornbush Abbey, from the stench of spinsterhood, the Most Revered Lord James, Earl of Jones, entailed his entire Nottinghamshire property to his third cousin, once removed, and her husband, should his only niece and heiress remain yet unmarried one year after his death. All interested parties were informed of this provision at Lord James's passing, and they now gathered in the solicitor's office on the one-year anniversary of that gentleman's death.

The lord's solicitor, Mr. Littlejohn, presided over the proceedings. He addressed the would-be heiress, Lady Robyn Hoode.

"It is a truth universally acknowledged that all women over the age of fourteen need the guidance of a husband in financial and moral matters. For this reason, Lord James deemed it necessary that you inherit his estate only if you married within the year subsequent to his passing. Have you?" the solicitor inquired.

Mrs. Forrester, the Lord's third cousin, smiled smugly at the question, proud of her married state and prejudiced against any alternative lifestyles.

"Have I?" Lady Robyn innocently repeated. She fully comprehended what was asked of her, but wished to embarrass the solicitor by forcing him to further expound.

"Ahem." The solicitor cleared his throat, blushed, and plainly asked the question, "Have you married?"

"If you mean, have I complied with my uncle's preposterous request, then the answer is no. I have long since been determined that I should not be prevailed upon to marry were I the last woman on earth solely responsible for the propagation of the entire species!"

The third cousin smiled wryly. The solicitor paused.

The pause was too long for Mrs. Forrester. "Well? Out with it!" she said. "No need to look so sour. I demand to know the value of my inheritance."

Again, the solicitor turned scarlet and tugged at his collar. "The fact of the matter is that in order for the property to be of any value, you will have to pay off the debts first. In truth, if you do not discharge the debts soon, your own assets may be in jeopardy."

Lady Robyn let out a peal of raucous laughter.

The third cousin once removed was not amused. She turned to her relative and thus abused her. "Insolent, greedy girl! Impudent upstart! I insist that you accept what is legally yours!"

"Legally mine? Not a bit of it. I believe that you are most deserving of what you have received," Lady Robyn rejoined, with no effort to conceal her obvious amusement.

"I will endure no more of your insults," Mrs. Forrester said, and turned to her husband. "This is your fault!" she scolded and then stormed out of the room with a huff and a puff. Before following, Mr. Forrester stole a glance at Lady Robyn, who was, at this moment, fiscally and physically more attractive to him than his wife.

After the Forresters had departed, Mr. Littlejohn congratulated the lord's niece on her decision. "I believe you have been prudent, though your uncle would not have agreed."

"My uncle lived in a different century. I can hardly credit his opinions."

Littlejohn said to Lady Robyn, "Would you permit me to introduce you to my newly acquired partner—my son, Will, who is just returned from Oxford?" he asked, solicitous for her acquiescence.

Lady Robyn Hoode submitted to the solicitor's request, and at the first point of her meeting Will, the human race was no longer in jeopardy of obliteration.

DID YOU KNOW?

Lacking most of the forms of amusement with which we entertain ourselves today, the lively, imaginative Austen children added something more ambitious to the usual books, musical performances, and card games that might have entertained their contemporaries during an evening at home: amateur theatricals. James, the eldest son and a serious writer, composed the prologues and epilogues for their performances of plays ranging from fine comedy to melodramatic tragedy. Richard Sheridan's *The Rivals* and Henry Fielding's *Tom Thumb* are examples of the former, Thomas Francklin's *Matilda* of the latter. One Christmas they even turned the barn into a real theater—meaning one with painted scenery—and continued to put on new plays even after the holiday.

∽ Finer Endings ∽
JENNIFER HESTER

Note: In addition to the anonymity with which Ms. Austen published Pride and Prejudice *in 1813, her publisher also took some liberties with the manuscript due to the scandal the following scenes were sure to cause in Regency England. These scenes were altered to a more befitting state. The original text, written in Ms. Austen's own hand, was only recently discovered. —JH.*

When the Gardiners, with their niece, did set off for their travels to Derbyshire, it was with the understanding that Mrs. Gardiner would help her sister, Mrs. Bennet, to find Elizabeth a husband. Mrs. Gardiner was well aware that, within five miles of her former residence in Lambton, set the estate of a most appealing match: Mr. Darcy of Pemberley, with £30,000 a year, who was, as fortune would have it, an acquaintance of the young lady. After squelching the objections of Elizabeth to see the place, Mrs. Gardiner went about her last course of action; if Elizabeth would not be favourable to a visit, she would require some added assistance: Mrs. Gardiner's Potion for Fine Endings. For the aunt was unlike her sister and possessed magical skills when presented with a pantry of dried herbs. Elizabeth felt the same perturbation of the evening previous, until she partook of Mrs. Gardiner's tea.

"This is delicious, Aunt. Did the herbs come from thine own garden?"

"Indeed they did, my dear Lizzy." Mrs. Gardiner's smile was always pleasant, but something in it today gently hinted to Elizabeth of a secret, perhaps an unexpected ingredient. Before there was time to inquire, Mr. Gardiner returned with news that their carriage had arrived. As they bumped along the ride to Pemberley Park, Mrs. Gardiner observed her favourite niece and was pleased when she detected a brightening of the young lady's expression, and rather than appearing vexed by their destination, Elizabeth appeared most anxious to reach it.

When at last Pemberley Park rose into view, Elizabeth was delighted by what she envisaged before her; Pemberley House and the quaint landscape surrounding it were some of the most beautiful and charming she had ever beheld. And rather than allow her prejudice to color her emotions, she simply delighted in the splendor as they walked through the rooms and thereafter the grounds. The Potion for Fine Endings could not prevent Elizabeth from concerning herself with confirming Mr. Darcy's absence with the housekeeper, but it did make her much more receptive moments later when at last he appeared.

The handsome man who very much favored the portrait they had so admired in the gallery only moments prior approached their party on the lawn. Elizabeth could not comprehend the feelings that came over her as she gazed upon Mr. Darcy's countenance that first time at Pemberley Park. Her aunt's tea seemed to bubble from within, and she felt shame at the embarrassment that seemed likely should she show behavior most unbecoming of a proper lady, particularly in the presence of a gentleman. The second feeling, which increasingly became more intense and unexpected, was the warmth in her chest, her face, the tingling of her hand as if it recalled that which was thrilling about his touch that day so long ago when he, being a proper if indifferent gentleman, had handed her into the carriage at Netherfield. She had never known such an effect on her being prior to this moment. Could it be that she loved him as he had so professed to love her only a short time ago at Rosings?

Mrs. Gardiner observed the state in which her dear Lizzy stood before Mr. Darcy of Pemberley. A slow smile spread across her face, for this niece she so loved was certain to be given an offer of marriage that she would most ardently accept. Mrs. Bennet would also be most pleased, and Mrs. Gardiner would be grateful to find a replacement for her sister's abundant complaints about unmarried daughters with praise over a most advantageous match.

Just one cup of tea, that's all the assistance dear Lizzy required, Mrs. Gardiner thought affectionately, patting her pocket full of secret herbs. A fine ending it was, indeed.

⌒ Miss Dashwood Gets Down and Dirty ⌒
SHANNON WINSLOW

"How long has this engagement of Edward's been known to you?" Marianne demanded.

"About four months," Elinor rejoined.

"What?! And never a hint to your closest companions?"

"No doubt you would reproach me again for my reserve and quarrel with me over my forbearance. Would you question the existence of my heart as well because I choose to suffer my disappointment in private?"

"Indeed, I do not ask the location of your heart, for I vouchsafe that you have an organ of that description beating within your breast, and it may well be as susceptible to tender sentiments as any other person's. My question to you, Elinor, is this: Where is your fighting spirit? You have been grossly ill-used, and the time to take decisive action is come!"

"I admire your conviction, dearest, but what recourse is there within my reach? The courts can give no satisfaction; no law has been broken. What would you have me do? Challenge Lucy Steele to a duel?"

"A tempting notion, is it not?" Marianne sprang into a fencer's stance and addressed a phantom rival with the cut and thrust of her imaginary saber.

"Marianne! Have you completely taken leave of your senses? Surely there can be no occasion for bloodshed."

"Perhaps not, but I have heard of another equally satisfactory avenue for settling disputes." Marianne clasped her sister's hand. "Come, make haste!"

Her protestations notwithstanding, Elinor found herself unceremoniously dragged to her feet and from the room. Marianne was unstoppable. She collected their wraps and propelled them both out into the street, where they were fortunate to find a hansom cab standing at liberty.

"Where to, Miss?" the cabbie asked as the young ladies climbed in.

"Southwark. To Vauxhall, and don't spare the horses," Marianne ordered. They were off with the crack of the driver's whip.

Elinor, who had been carried thus far by the sheer force of her sister's will, at last spoke out. "I must protest against this madness, Marianne. You intend to take us across the river and into the Borough at this time of night? And unescorted? Only think what our mother would say to such a scheme!"

"Mama need never know. Besides, it would be well worth any price for the chance to see you settle your score with Lucy. It was, in fact, by overhearing her speak of the contest tonight that I learnt of it myself. According to her information, this form of entertainment is quite the thing here in London now, so you need not be squeamish."

Her scruples laid to rest by these reassuring words, Elinor's mind eased from concern to mere curiosity. As long as no breach of decorum was involved, a new diversion would be welcome. One could not go to the opera every night of the week, after all. But how a Vauxhall amusement could render any amendment to a broken heart, Elinor could not begin to fathom.

"Be patient," Marianne answered when asked. "You will see soon enough."

Elinor's bewilderment only increased upon their arrival, however, for she heard sounds of a great tumult emanating from the vast tent to which her sister steered her.

"This cannot be entirely proper," she said. "Ladies and gentleman never raise their voices in such a manner at the theatre or at a ball."

Marianne pressed ahead, taking no notice. Another moment and they were both within the canvas enclosure, hemmed about on all sides by crowds of unruly persons, many of whom were of dubious lineage. Elinor stood transfixed for a long moment, not believing her eyes. "B-but Marianne, those t-two young ladies . . ." Elinor pushed forward for a better view. "They seem to be . . ."

"Yes, they are indeed!" Marianne confirmed. "Glorious, is it not?"

DID YOU KNOW?

James Austen, the eldest Austen son, ten years older than Jane, had established himself as the writer in the family long before Jane could have been taken very seriously as such. He was always a good scholar, attended Oxford, and, like his father, was ordained in the Church of England. In 1789, after the verse prologues and epilogues for the family theatricals were behind him, he began publishing his own weekly magazine, *The Loiterer*. It was modeled after Samuel Johnson's important and wonderful periodicals, *The Rambler* and *The Idler*. Henry, another brother, also contributed to it. *The Loiterer* was published for fourteen months and distributed in London, Oxford, and other major towns in England. In later life James continued to write poetry for the pleasure of his family, but if he had any greater ambition for his writing beyond that, it was unrealized.

"I hardly know. I would not have imagined such a thing possible . . . or prudent," Elinor murmured, tilting her head this way and that as she followed the movements of the female contenders. An inner voice whispered that she should be repulsed, that she ought to turn on her heel and flee the den of iniquity at once. Yet she found that she could not; she was irresistibly drawn to the spectacle before her. The singular visage of Lucy Steele suddenly appeared amongst the onlookers across the way, and, when their eyes met, Elinor shot her a pointed look through the steamy atmosphere betwixt them. Lucy nodded, accepting the silent challenge. As if by some audible signal, they started toward each other at the very same moment. The crowd cheered, apprehending that some considerable augmentation to the evening's entertainment was forthcoming. With an expression of exhilaration overspreading her countenance, Elinor cast caution to the wind, hoisted up her skirts, and waded into the mud-filled arena to meet her adversary.

⌁ The Perilous Plot at Pemberley ⌁
Patti Wigington

It was a dark and stormy night. Our hired carriage broke down on the side of the road ten miles from Pemberley. The driver, fearful of the lightning and thunder, ran off into the darkness.

My darling Freddie suggested I stay with the coach while he went for help. I had not long to wait, for shortly he returned in a second carriage, driven by a disheveled young man. Frederick assisted me into this conveyance and explained that the lady within was also headed to Pemberley.

"I am Georgiana Fitzwilliam," I said, "and you have met my husband, Colonel Fitzwilliam."

"I am Miss Dinkley," she said, blinking through a pair of thick spectacles. "I am to be governess to the Darcy daughters."

Before I could reply, I was nudged by something damp. I nearly leapt from my seat, startled as I was.

"Oh," Miss Dinkley laughed, "pay no mind. Mr. Rodgers, the coachman, has brought his dog with him. He answers to Scoobert. I have treats in my reticule, if you would like to offer him a snack."

We soon arrived at Pemberley. The storm had worsened, and Freddie recommended the coachman spend the night rather than venture back to his village. He readily agreed, and we left him and his dog indulging in a plate of mutton in the kitchens. It was a joy to see my brother and Lizzie after our years in India. Their daughters, Charlotte and Catherine, were abed, but we spent hours catching up on news of the surrounding countryside. It was good to see familiar faces; Lizzie's sister Jane and her husband, Bingley, were there, as were Bingley's sister, Caroline, and Mr. and Mrs. Collins of Rosings Park.

After everyone retired for the evening, Lizzie took me aside. "Georgiana," she said, "I confess, I am troubled. I feel foolish speaking of this, but you know Pemberley much better than I. Is it possible—dare I ask—could Pemberley be haunted?"

I laughed despite myself. "It is possible, but I have never—why Lizzie! You are white as a sheet! What has happened?"

"Georgiana, it is awful! There is a terrible spectre! I have seen it three nights in a row, outside my rooms, wailing and howling! It says I must leave Pemberley at once!"

I frowned. "It speaks to you?"

She nodded. "I have said nothing to your brother; Fitz is such a skeptic. And yet I feel there is something truly wrong here. I am certain I am being watched, even when I am alone."

I patted her hand. "I shall speak to Freddie of this, and we shall solve the mystery. Worry no more."

As I climbed into bed, I told my husband of Lizzie's fears. Despite his being fifteen years my senior, Freddie never dismissed me as frivolous, and so he concurred we must do what we could to help. We agreed to take turns listening in the night.

Much later, Freddie woke me. "A noise in the hall," he whispered. I scurried to the door and eased it open. The corridor was dark.

We tiptoed slowly down the hall, and then I too heard a sound. As we rounded a corner, I gasped. "Miss Dinkley!"

"I heard a noise," she said softly, "but now I cannot find my room again. You see, I've lost my glasses."

There was another footfall, and Mr. Rodgers and Scoobert appeared. "What ho?" he asked. "I was looking for a midnight snack, and—"

"Hush!" I whispered. "Look!"

At the far end of the corridor, away from the shadows where we were concealed, a ghostly figure glided up to Lizzie's door.

"Wooooooo!" it moaned. "Leeeeeeeeavvvve this hoooooooouse! Woooooooo!"

"Yikes!" exclaimed Rodgers. Miss Dinkley squinted toward the sound, and Freddie and I ran down the hall at the gauzy gray spectre. Suddenly, Scoobert raced in front of me, and I tripped over his paws, toppling straight into the apparition!

Which let out a feminine squeal and some very bad words.

I reached up and pulled the filmy veil from the ghost's head and was all astonishment.

"Caroline Bingley!" exclaimed Miss Dinkley, Mr. Rodgers, and Freddie.

"Yes," she spat. "It is I who should be mistress of Pemberley! And I would have gotten away with it, too, if it hadn't been for you meddling—"

"What is the meaning of this?" my brother roared, appearing behind us. I explained all to him and Lizzie, and to the Bingleys and Collinses as well, who had awakened at the commotion. Caroline was banished to her room by a very angry Lizzie.

Miss Dinkley handed me a treat, which I passed to Scoobert.

"After all," I exclaimed, "he helped us unmask the poltergeist of Pemberley!"

⌁ Pride and Prejudice: The First Draft ⌁
GLORIA GAY

A want of discretion propelled Mrs. Bennet to Netherfield Park through inclement weather. Mrs. Bennet surmised she would be ensconced at the Hall during the cold she would catch and Jane would visit, establishing an occasion for Jane to bring Mr. Bingley up to scratch. Mrs. Bennet took not even her Abigail with her, for she was certain her married status protected her from bad taste and even worse manners.

It was a locally acknowledged truth that there were few bachelors in the vicinity and even fewer eligible ones. But a maiden such as the beauteous Jane, who had a maternal parent such as Mrs. Bennet, had a definite advantage, for Mrs. Bennet had a tendency to count the chickens before the hen had even glanced at the rooster.

Mr. Darcy had made it apparent at the Netherfield Ball that no access to his friend, Mr. Bingley, and his fortune was forthcoming. This was to Mrs. Bennet the opening volley in a battle of wits, which she had no intention of losing, no matter that her nerves were, as usual, in poor condition.

The door was opened by Mr. Darcy, of whom Mrs. Bennet had heard ill reports. A shiver of apprehension ran through her with such dizzying force she swooned toward him, and had not Mr. Darcy, who had in his hand a volume he had been of late perusing, stopped her fall, she would have toppled him to the floor.

"Madam," said Mr. Darcy coldly, "comport yourself."

"I have been accosted by inclement weather on my way to Netherfield to call on Mr. Bingley and caught cold," said Mrs. Bennet as she fell on a nearby couch in a studied pose.

"Mr. Bingley is from home," said Mr. Darcy, his voice dripping icicles, which was rather upsetting to Mrs. Bennet, especially since, as she was prone on the couch, Mr. Darcy was forced to look down on her even more than he had looked down at her at the assembly ball.

"I am unable to return by the same way," said Mrs. Bennet, sneezing loudly. "I must apply to Miss Bingley to attend to me. Please fetch her, Mr. Darcy."

Miss Bingley had for some time held a pose in a tableau of her own design in the library, but Mr. Darcy had not come by to enjoy it, so she had gone about the house looking for him. Then Miss Bingley heard the commotion in the front hall and headed quickly toward it. She shook her head in disgust.

"What is this, an invasion of Barrets, Mr. Darcy?"

Miss Bingley was dressed in a shade of green as unbecoming as her complexion, which was of a puce tint that spread throughout her face, even under her abnormally small ears.

"Miss Bingley," said Mrs. Bennet, "I must appeal to you. Having been caught in the rain, I am unable to leave for at least a fortnight, while I allow you good people to nurse me through la grippe."

"Mama!" Lizzy had just been allowed in by the butler of Netherfield Hall and stood aghast as she gazed at her mother, prone on the couch.

"Lizzy! What are you doing here, child? It is Jane I told the maid to send to me. You are not needed here."

"Mr. Darcy!" Lizzy glanced at Mr. Darcy in alarm.

Mr. Darcy noticed that Miss Elizabeth Bennet's complexion had altered to a vivid red, which was not altogether to his disgust.

He remembered that at the Netherfield Ball the night before he had disdained dancing with her, so he hurried to make amends.

"I would as soon allow you the privilege of dancing with me than not, Miss Elizabeth," Mr. Darcy assured her.

"I would as soon you didn't than did, Mr. Darcy," said Lizzy firmly. "I overheard you tell Mr. Bingley that my sister's prospects and even less pedigree would be demeaning to him," she added.

"I was merely stating the obvious," said Mr. Darcy, instantly regretting his words as he perused her reaction to them. Mr. Darcy tried to remove Miss Bingley's long fingers from his arm as he spoke. "I was certain my treatment of Wickham was what most upset you, Miss Elizabeth."

"I cannot easily forget that either, Mr. Darcy," said Lizzy.

"Miss Elizabeth, Wickham's primary concern in life is the improvement of his bank account, which he would attain by marriage."

"Perchance you would wed me yourself, Mr. Darcy?" asked Lizzy. "Well, this is what I say to that: I would rather kiss a frog and marry it than walk down the aisle with you!"

"Do you mean to say, Miss Elizabeth," said Mr. Darcy, quite dazed, "that you have considered marriage to me?"

⌒ Christmas at Pemberley ⌒
DIANA L. GRANGER

The Darcys greeted the Bennets dutifully as they arrived to spend Christmas at Pemberley. Not to extend familial hospitality would show a want of breeding.

Mrs. Bennet clasped Elizabeth in a fond embrace. "Darling Lizzie, how good to see you and how fine you look." She continued on, barely acknowledging Mr. Darcy, the source of that felicitous fortune.

Following in the wake of Mrs. Bennet were Mr. Bennet and daughter Mary. Mary lacked the charms so admired by the young bucks of society. Alas, even Mrs. Bennet was reconciled to this daughter remaining a spinster.

Mary retired to her chamber after learning that tea would be served at four. Later there would be Christmas Eve services in the private family chapel.

After freshening up, Mary sought out the famous Pemberley library. She entered the spacious book-lined room. As she stood there, awestruck, a young man asked politely, "May I help you, miss?"

"A muse has surely directed my steps hither to this repository of wisdom. I'm Mary Bennet, sister of Mrs. Darcy," Mary announced. "I'm here for Christmas."

"It's a pleasure to meet you, Miss Bennet. I'm Raymond Atherton, and I'm cataloguing the Pemberley library. I would be most gratified to show you its marvels," the young bespectacled man said brightly. Compared with the patrician good looks of Mr. Darcy, Raymond Atherton seemed unremarkable. His nose was too pointed and his legs too thin. When he spoke, his Adam's apple coursed up and down his neck; however, he had the kindest smile Mary had ever seen.

"To misquote Shakespeare," Mary intoned, "knowing you loved his books, he furnished you from his own library with volumes—"

"—that I prize above his kingdom." Mr. Atherton completed the altered phrase from *The Tempest* and laughed appreciatively.

Mary had never felt as comfortable with any new acquaintance as with this affable young man who seemed so delighted with her companionship. Too soon the gong sounded, calling guests to tea.

"I fear I must defer the pleasure of discovering the treasures herein housed." Disappointment infused her words.

"Likely, I'll see you at services tonight. Father is rector here," Mr. Atherton called out.

At tea, Mrs. Bennet ate happily of the delicacies before her and used the opportunity to decry the state of public transportation. Mary was unusually quiet, and Elizabeth wondered why.

Later the family processed to the Darcy chapel. The rector entered, accompanied by Raymond bearing the gilded Darcy Bible. Raymond beamed when he saw Mary, and she in return smiled radiantly back at him. Both mother and sister noted this exchange.

Early Christmas morning, Elizabeth wrote a missive to Mrs. Atherton to request their company at the Darcy table.

At breakfast Mr. Darcy assured Mrs. Bennet that the Athertons were persons of quality. "Young Raymond graduated from

Cambridge and has excellent prospects. He loves our library, so for now he has the cataloguing responsibility."

Dinner conversation was not about French politics, grouse shooting, or epicurean delights, but was rather a duel of doting mothers. Both matriarchs described paragons of virtue.

Did You Know?

In 1790, when Jane was just fourteen, she dedicated an ambitious burlesque of a certain type of popular writing, the so-called sentimental novel, to her cousin Eliza. Jane called it a novel, but it is little more than story length, consisting of a series of letters in which fifty-five-year-old Laura tells the story of her life to Marianne, the young daughter of a friend, purportedly as an admonitory tale. *Love and Freindship* (yes, Jane spelled it that way) is absolutely hilarious, and Austen fans who have read only her novels have another great (if quite short) treat awaiting them.

Austen's early writing is very much focused on mocking the contemporary vogue for what she saw as absurdly unrealistic literature. She had an easy target in the sentimental novel, in which extreme emotional responses—both on the part of the characters and, presumably, the readers—were relentlessly manifested. Rational thought is very little in evidence and, indeed, is disdained. Austen also takes spirited delight in writing humorously about violence and the grossly immoral and illegal behavior of the characters.

After dinner the two who were being extolled slipped away, roaming through the fabulous halls of Pemberley, ending up in the library. Mary addressed Raymond passionately, "I would love to aid you in your cataloguing."

Raymond responded, "How transfixed with pleasure I would be with you copying beside me."

"My handwriting is rather good," Mary asserted. Raymond took her hand and kissed it. "Sweet hand that writes so well. I think in its palm I'll find my destiny."

So the Darcys now had two cataloguers scribbling away happily.

As the Bennets were leaving, Mrs. Bennet approached Mr. Darcy warmly. "Thank you for this Christmas. You have given me the best gift a mother can receive, a suitable matrimonial candidate for her spinster daughter!"

Meekness and Misery; or, The Sad Love Affair of Mary Bennet
DIANE KATHERINE HOSTERMAN

Mary Bennet gazed into the reflecting mirror; her thin, wispy hair had been tortured into a pile of wan curls on her head. The effect led her to one conclusion: Not only was she not a Greek goddess, she was—as was whispered behind fans in various assemblies around the neighborhood—"not the equal in beauty to any of her sisters." She had heard it all her life and had decided that a quickness of wit and other womanly accomplishments were her gifts and highly prized by society. At least that's what she continued to tell herself every time she saw evidence to the contrary.

With Lizzy's unfathomable declination of Mr. Collins's proposal, Mary finally saw her chance to capture his attention. Tonight she would delight Mr. Collins with several turns at the piano and flatter him by asking him to read aloud for the benefit of her mind. She didn't feel her mind needed much more cultivation, but a man as learned as Mr. Collins would appreciate a woman listening intently and whose mind was focused more on the improvement of manners in a civilized society instead of the latest fashion in bonnets.

Mary considered the satisfaction she would feel when she married first; when she was finally treated as the heroine she was; when she—plain, insignificant, overlooked Mary Bennet—saved Longbourn from being entailed away. Oh, she could see the envious and grateful looks of her sisters as she marched down the aisle, on her way to becoming Mrs. Collins. How they would fawn over her for saving them from destitution. How her mother would dote over her. Then she would become her mother's favorite instead of that vapid Lydia.

She rose from her dressing table and picked up a half-finished floral pillow cover to use as a substitute bouquet. With her head held high, her bedroom became a church; the window seat, a pew. There was Jane, beautiful, ethereal Jane. The look of gratitude on her sister's face made up for all the dances Jane was asked for that Mary was not. She acknowledged her sister with a nod of her head. And there, sitting next to Jane was Elizabeth. *Yes, that's right, Elizabeth. You turned him down; now watch me marry the only man who will ever propose to you.*

Elizabeth was looking down, holding her handkerchief to her eyes. Was she crying? Or was she laughing? Poor Lizzy, this could have been her wedding day and now she regretted her decision. Madness would be her lifelong companion. Mary pitied her and glanced at her with worry.

In Kitty's eyes she saw . . . boredom? Poor Kitty, her attention had never been captured by anything for long. She smiled condescendingly at her. Lydia looked at her mischievously; perhaps she was imagining her future walk down the aisle. Mary smiled at her simple sister; after all, she wasn't a horrid person, just flighty. She could hear her mother weeping with joy.

Mary's reverie was interrupted by a sharp rap on the door. She threw the embroidery back to its workspace as the maid announced supper. Her heart quickened at the thought of the proximity she would soon have to her beloved Mr. Collins, but she managed a dignified walk down the stairs to her appointed seat at the table. She sat down with an interior excitement that no one at the table suspected—then with horror noticed that her Mr. Collins was not there.

The tenseness at the table was disturbed by Mrs. Bennet's occasional exclamations of "Charlotte Lucas! Charlotte Lucas!" Mr. Bennet did not even try to calm or comfort her. Mary was confounded by her mother's behavior until Kitty whispered to her that Mr. Collins had become engaged to Charlotte Lucas that afternoon and was dining at Lucas Lodge that evening.

Alas, she did not whisper softly enough, and that set Mrs. Bennet off on another round of exclamations and up to her room with a headache. Mr. Bennet continued to enjoy his dinner, and his daughters managed to uphold a pleasant, if not exactly lively, conversation.

Mary was lost in the indignity of it all. How could they just go on? Did they not know she had just lost the love of her life? The outrage! The stunning outrage! Just a few moments ago, she was on her way to being the savior of her sisters, and now she was back to being ignored; certainly no one at the supper table had noticed her agitation. No one at the supper table noticed her at all.

John & Rebeccah:
A Tale of Love Midst the Stars
CHERYL ANGST

It should be noted that John Thompson, formerly a lecturer of distinction and more recently a captain in the fleet, being a widower these many years and having become exceedingly set in his solitary ways, placed little stock in the attentions of the fairer sex. Thus, it came as quite a shock to his disposition to discover not one, but two women vying for his affections—however atrophied and unpractised those affections might now be.

Miss Rebeccah Santiago, whose skill with the written word made angelic melodies of the driest ration cutlery reports, possessed the most remarkable green eyes, and Mr. Thompson experienced the stirrings of emotions long buried whenever she turned her sparkling orbs on him. And, to his great surprise, she seemed to regard his slate ones with similar interest.

Miss Miller, the other young woman pursuing the esteemed captain, while demonstrating many outward signs of being well-bred and a desirable helpmeet for any man fortunate enough to attract her eye, was, in fact, mean in both thought and action, regarding her fellow officers as trappings to be used and discarded as necessary. And from Miss Miller's perspective, Mr. Thompson represented the Sunday-best bonnet in the wardrobe of her life.

Despite Miss Miller's brash attempts to entice the captain, Mr. Thompson's burgeoning feelings of warmth and desire were firmly directed at Miss Rebeccah. However, Miss Rebeccah had yet to discern Mr. Thompson's mind in the matter of his heart, and she fretted, although, as the second in command, she would deny such actions most vehemently and conspired to determine the true nature of Mr. Thompson's regard once and for all.

"Sir," Miss Rebeccah said, "if I may, I would like a word with you." She paused in her request and glanced pointedly at Miss Miller. "In private."

"Of course," he replied and retired to his office, attributing the stuttering of his heart to Miss Rebeccah's increasing influence over his being.

"Sir," said Rebeccah, "I am concerned you do not view me in the way I wish to be perceived, and I feel compelled to rectify this matter immediately."

Mr. Thompson was taken aback. Had he misinterpreted her intentions from the outset? He shook his head and apologized.

"No, sir," she replied, "I do not desire your culpability, but rather to hear, in your own words, precisely how you see me, as an officer and, more importantly, as a woman."

Fearing he could lose one of the most capable executive officers he'd had the pleasure of serving with if he misspoke, he couched his answer in terms of her professional qualities and stayed as far as possible from describing how her beauty and wit entranced him.

Miss Rebeccah sidled closer to the captain, frustrated by his avoidance of the more personal aspect of her request. "That is all well and good, sir, but," she said, stepping near, so near that if she inhaled deeply, her uniform must surely brush his, "what are your views on me as a member of the opposite sex?"

Heat raced up Thompson's neck, burning his ears and setting his cheeks aflame. How she affected him! Her eyes, such green eyes, held him captive and a slave to her will, and he, he acknowledged without regret, wished to remain imprisoned for the rest of his mortal life.

Rebeccah started as his lips pressed into hers. Her heart, skittering as it was with apprehension, threatened to escape her chest as the truth of his feelings for her became readily apparent. She permitted him to draw her more deeply into his embrace and fought down her own rising desire when he ceased his tender display of tonguesmanship.

"You are the most remarkable woman I have ever had the acquaintance of," said Thompson. "My darling, you complete my soul, and I would rather be tossed out an air lock than spend another minute living without you."

Rebeccah leaned in and kissed Thompson again.

She stepped back, heart full to bursting, when he asked, "Have I made myself sufficiently clear?"

Rebeccah, confident in the rightness of their love, replied, "Perfectly, Captain. I am exceedingly relieved we had this discussion. Now that we understand one another, I feel as though a great weight has been lifted from my shoulders."

"I fear it has been some time since I last courted," said Thompson. "You may find my efforts fail to meet your expectations."

"I don't need you to pitch woo, Mr. Thompson," said she. "Our love for one another, freely acknowledged here, is adequate assurance that your affections are genuine."

Captain Thompson marveled at the woman standing before him. His life of solitary contemplation ended the moment he took her into his arms, and, like the beckoning stars beyond the viewports, he would follow both to the ends of the universe.

⌐ Pride and Predictions ⌐
KRISTINE HUDSON

Elizabeth Bennet sat at the table in complete expectancy. "My mother says that you are the very best occultist. You can see the future just as we look out the window to see the day's weather."

The occultist Celeste nodded her head and smiled gently. "Yes, your mother is correct. What is the question of your heart?"

"Who is the man I will marry?" Elizabeth asked. Her voice trembled slightly.

Celeste turned several tarot cards face-up. Elizabeth could not tell from her expression if the future was sunny or cloudy.

"There is a man in your life now. One with great charm," Celeste said. She pointed to the King of Cups. The card was upside down. "My dear, this man is not true to you in his words and deeds."

Elizabeth gasped; a hand went over her face. "Mr. Wickham is kind and decent. He is a lieutenant."

Celeste pointed to the card next to it, the King of Swords. "There is another man, dark-haired and quite energetic. This is a man who is true to his words. I see a marriage with him motivated by love and not convenience. However, this King of Swords has said words that wounded you in the past?"

Darcy. Tears came to Elizabeth's eyes. She shook her head vehemently. "No, you are wrong. Something is terribly wrong. I agree that the dark-haired man has been hurtful, but I have no desire to marry him. There is no desire from him as well."

Celeste tipped back her head and laughed, deep and cackling. "The cards do not lie. Destiny does not lie. Fate does not tell us tall tales. This man," Celeste pointed to the card again. "Darcy is the one you will marry. And you will desire this marriage just as deeply as he does!"

Did You Know?

Although drafts of the novels that would become *Pride and Prejudice* and *Sense and Sensibility* were written earlier, Austen does not seem to have revised *Northanger Abbey* much after 1803—whereas she did revise the others after moving to Chawton—and so *Northanger Abbey* is generally considered her earliest novel. A first draft was written between 1798 and 1799, and some have argued that it was in fact begun four or five years earlier. But we do not have to look to extrinsic evidence to suspect that this high-spirited tale was a youthful work: The style seems to link it both to an earlier period of English history and an earlier period in Austen's development. It is closer in some ways to the juvenilia than it is to the mature novels. Finally, Austen herself asserts that it was the work of an earlier time.

Like so much of her juvenilia, *Northanger Abbey* satirizes contemporary taste in literature, in particular the rage for Gothic novels. It is, in a way, a novel about books. Its self-conscious "literariness" is reinforced by the frequent authorial intrusions in which the narrator discusses her "heroine" in the context of what heroines usually are and usually do. It is actually the false Isabella who imitates with precision the heroines of the novels Austen found so preposterously unreal. She proclaims to Catherine (whose brother's fortune will be very modest), "Had I the command of millions, were I mistress of the whole world, your brother would be my only choice" and, we are told, "This charming sentiment, recommended as much by sense as novelty, gave Catherine a most pleasing remembrance of all the heroines of her acquaintance." But there is not an ounce of sincerity in Isabella's pronouncement of this "grand idea," and the heroine ideal perpetuated by Gothic novels is equally—and laughably—false in Austen's view.

Elizabeth blushed at her indecent remark. "Mr. Darcy does not . . . does not feel that way about me. He wouldn't even dance with me a single time. Why, Mr. Darcy is not an honorable man," Elizabeth finished with a sigh.

Celeste pointed to the final card. The Wheel of Fortune. "Give it time, my sweet child, give it time. This love will bloom."

"I'm afraid you are incorrect. Mr. Darcy shows no interest in me. There will be no love blooming between the two of us," Elizabeth retorted.

The final card was turned over. The Ten of Pentacles. "My dear, a single man in possession of a good fortune must be in want of a wife," Celeste replied gently. "This man is good, true and kind, and also possesses great fortune. But you hesitate as you lack this same good fortune."

Elizabeth met her gaze. "Mr. Darcy is none of these things that you tell me, except for possessing great fortune. However, should this fortune matter greatly, then I would prefer not to be acquainted with him, thank you very much!" Elizabeth rose to leave.

Her mother was waiting outside, tapping her foot impatiently.

"Well, did she promise a betrothal?" Her mother demanded. The refusal of Mr. Collins was simply too much for her to bear.

"These occultists are foolish nonsense," Elizabeth replied. "They will say anything for a few coins."

Of Turbans, Partridges, and Apple Pie
THE JANITE

FITZWILLIAM DARCY to CHARLES BINGLEY
—St., London. Sunday (September 1, 1811)

My dear Charles,

I had the good fortune of reacquainting myself with your Sister two weeks ago & was very pleased to find little alteration had taken place in her disposition: She is still excessively proud of her Modesty and Humility. It is, however, my sad Fate having to inform you of an unhappy accident that took place mere minutes after I had asked Caroline for her hand. Her newly acquired red Turban, adorned with a vast array of peacock feathers & about as big as the neck of Miss ___ is fat, unfortunately toppled from her head as consequence of a burst of laughter & happily made the acquaintance of several partridges and an apple tart.

The ensuing mortification seemed to silence her (& I daresay she shall not ever be prevailed upon to relate both the preceding & following Tale), but she was at length forced to speak by Miss Mary Crawford—whose wit & easy manners you must surely remember from our last stay in Town—who assured her that being exposed is "all the rage in some districts of London"; she entreated us not to suspect her of a pun, but alas! the damage had been done & I fear we shall have to drop the acquaintance; pray tell me whether you can bear never to see those "fine eyes," as you once called them, again.

I remain, &c. &c.,

FITZWILLIAM DARCY.

CHARLES BINGLEY to CAROLINE BINGLEY
—shire. Tuesday (September 3, 1811)

My dear Caroline,

How sly you and Mr. Darcy are! Engaged indeed! I fear a lack of trust must have been the cause of this duplicitous secrecy, tho' it cd. not be kept from me for long; in what I fancy must have been a moment of carelessness he dropp'd a hint, for he told me he "asked Caroline for her hand," and cd. not anything be more obvious? Sister, imagine my surprise that he, [scratched out: who never seem'd to pay you any compliments of the sort] who never seemed interested in Matrimony, shd. [scratched out: prefer you over any other lady of our acquaintance!] finally have engaged himself! Yet I look forward to welcoming him as my brother, tho' I must confess it is a great disappointment that your engagement shall prevent you from keeping house for me when I take possession of Netherfield Park. I shall, however, bear this deprivation with Fortitude & wish you the utmost Joy & Felicity. Might one enquire when the Engagement is to be made Public & when the Ceremony is to take place?

I remain your affectionate brother, &c. &c.,
CHARLES BINGLEY.

CAROLINE BINGLEY to CHARLES BINGLEY
—St., London. Friday (September 6, 1811)

My dear Charles,

How I wish you would not write in the most careless way imaginable. You leave out half the words and blot all the rest; I daresay Mr. D., whose Brilliancy prevents him from writing unintelligibly, could teach you a lesson or two. Charles, you distress me by presuming I am engaged & I must assure you that nobody could be less inclined than myself to find herself in love with such a respectable, noble, amiable man with manners so fine, breeding so good & fortune so great! Nay, Charles, I positively declare it to be impossible & am all astonishment, tho' I am quite aware where the misunderstanding must have arisen from. A fortnight ago we received an invitation to a private ball and dinner held by the odious Miss Crawford (tho' you like her a great deal), which we gracefully & condescendingly accepted as there were no other amusements to be had; you know how dreadful it is for a single woman in possession of a good fortune to be locked up in one's house all day long without any prospect of forming new attachments. Mr. D. & I set off for the ball & found everyone dancing the quadrille. It would have been a punishment for Mr. D. to stand up with people he is not acquainted with; therefore he secured my hand for the first few dances. Pray believe me to be sincere, as I would never lie to you. I must now leave off writing this letter & give directions to the servants to wash my new turban, which a servant—through no fault of my own—accidentally splattered with Victuals. By the bye, you must forgive me for the sorry state this letter will arrive in: Tho' a less refined person than yourself, such as a certain Miss C., would undoubtedly concoct a witticism of sorts & say that it must have lain under a weeping willow for quite some time, I can assure you that these stains originate in nothing more serious than an accidental spillage of tea.

I remain your affectionate sister, &c. &c.,
CAROLINE BINGLEY.

Did You Know?

Jane Austen began writing a novel she called *First Impressions* in October 1796, when she was "not one and twenty," as Elizabeth Bennet puts it. It was completed in August of the following year.

By this time it was customary for Jane to entertain her family with her writing, and we can only imagine how she must have delighted them with this effort!

Mr. Austen, good, supportive father—and excellent reader—that he was, thought enough of Jane's story to seek to have it published. On November 1, 1797—losing no time—he sent it to the publisher Thomas Cadell in London with a highly respectful letter asking if Cadell would consider publishing it. Mr. Austen didn't reveal the author's name, but simply compared the length of the manuscript with that of Fanny Burney's 1778 novel in letters, *Evelina*. He even offered to risk his own money to see his daughter's work published.

Well, Mr. Austen could not have received a faster, curter, or—as history has shown—dumber reply: "Declined by return of post."

Luckily for the world, that wasn't the end of *First Impressions*—but it would still be many years before anyone outside Austen's inner circle would read the novel. It was not published until 1813, after it had been "lop't and crop't" by its author. In the meantime, in 1800, a novel also called *First Impressions*, written by Margaret Holford, had been published, which probably prompted Austen to change the title of her book.

It is interesting to ask, along with Juliet, "What's in a name?" Would *Pride and Prejudice*—a book with that most famous of titles—be any different if we knew it instead as *First Impressions*?

⟶ Foolishness and Folly ⟶
PATTI WIGINGTON

Though in general he was a terrible gambler and had lost nearly everything he owned, and many things that he didn't, George Wickham had found himself on a lucky streak lately, and his brand new barouche, formerly the property of a Mr. Willoughby of Devonshire, had become Wickham's with the play of just a few discreetly hidden cards. Willoughby was quite low about the loss, but had tempered his poor luck with the knowledge that he would soon marry an as-yet-virginal young lady with £60,000.

Wickham stood outside the regimental headquarters in his fine red coat, the morning sun blazing upon his handsome dark curls, and rubbed a door panel with a soft bit of chamois. Seeing his own dashing reflection, he preened, but his attention was caught by a flash of lavender in his peripheral vision. Miss Lydia Bennet and her sister Kitty approached, taking their morning constitutional through Meryton so that they might enjoy the view of handsome soldiers in fine regimentals.

"Well, Mr. Wickham, whose fine barouche are you polishing?" Lydia exclaimed.

Wickham shrugged with some degree of feigned indifference. "This old thing? A gentleman practically begged me to take it. He had promised to donate a few pounds to a kitten rescue agency, you see, and found himself short. I had to think of the kittens, Miss Bennet."

Lydia clasped her hands to her breast. "Dear generous Wickham, the kittens! You are too good!"

Wickham slowly ran the chamois down the length of the barouche, rubbing it in slow, languorous circles. Was it possible that Lydia's breath had quickened just a bit?

Kitty scowled. "We have no use for kittens. Everyone knows we are quite mad about puppies. It is for puppies that we go simply wild. Kittens, indeed!"

"Never listen to Kitty, dear Wickham," Lydia cried. "Indeed, I always say there is nothing quite so handsome as a man with a collection of kittens in a fine gleaming barouche!"

"You say no such thing, and I shall tell Mama you are being vulgar," Kitty hissed. She stuck her tongue out at Lydia and retreated to the milliner's shop.

"Miss Lydia," said Wickham, sliding his fingers gracefully along the barouche's leather upholstery, "I have it from your sister Elizabeth that soon you shall be removed to Brighton as a guest of Mrs. Foster's. Is this mere rumor, or dare I hope to see you at the Assembly Rooms of that fine town?"

Lydia noticed his hand softly caressing the bright red seats of the barouche and felt her pulse begin to pound. Surely, all this talk of kittens and barouches could not be distracting her so! Why, just recently Lydia had actually taken the time to read a book—well, perhaps not really read, but skim over—and had found herself having to loosen her stays while perusing the description of a carriage being plundered by highwaymen. Why, just the memory of the word *plunder* made Lydia catch her breath a bit and feel somewhat tingly in parts of her body of which a lady never spoke.

Recollecting where she was, Lydia blushed prettily and regained her composure. "If my sister Lizzie tells you I am to go to Brighton, then it must be true, Mr. Wickham. I will indeed be in Brighton very soon."

Wickham stepped back, noticing a tiny speck of dust on the side of the barouche, marring the vehicle's perfect appearance. "Oh dear. A spot. It cannot be borne, Miss Lydia. Do excuse me a moment." He leaned in close to the side of the barouche, opened his mouth, and exhaled warmly onto the speck. The gleaming wood, polished within an inch of its life, fogged at the heat of his breath, and when Wickham pressed his thumb to the warm spot and rubbed it gently, Lydia thought that she might faint right there on the street.

"Wickham," she gasped, a catch in her throat. "Will you come find me in Brighton?"

He glanced up at her, licking his lips gently. "Would you like that, Miss Bennet?"

She nodded, barely able to speak. "We could perhaps take a ride in your barouche."

"Indeed we could," he murmured, rising to his feet so that he could look down at her. "And perhaps, Miss Bennet, we could pay a visit to the kitten shelter."

Lydia closed her eyes and sighed, nearly weeping with joy. She knew that any resolve she might have had before this day would be lost, along with her virtue, the moment Wickham came for her in his barouche and took her to visit a houseful of kittens.

⌒ In a More Canine-Like Manner ⌒
TAMARA HANSON

Miss Basset was suddenly roused by the sound of the doorbell, and her spirits were a little shaken when after only two barks who should enter but Mr. Tabby. Her tail lay straight and still beside her, demonstrating the annoyance she felt to see him only sit and stare at nothing on the wall. She couldn't help but be curious at his behaviour. Just as she tilted her head and raised her eyebrows at him, he began:

"In vain have I tussled. It will not do. My feelings will not be repressed. You must have noticed the uncontrolled purring, the gazing at you, the slow blinks I have given you. When I greet you nose to nose, I have a strong urge to rub my face against yours and curl up beside you. Miss Basset, I must urge you to ease my suffering and consent to being my napping partner and mate."

Miss Basset's bewilderment was beyond expression. She had noticed him blankly staring at her before, but she had been taught that it was the way of his kind. Indeed, she was truly astonished. She paced in a circle, nipped at her sides, and made a low growling whine. She felt none of the great good luck he supposed she would be feeling to be addressed by one with such a pedigree.

She did not bark or snap at him, so he continued: "You must see the aversion I have had to come to this conclusion. In doing so I know I am insulting myself, alienating my family, even going against nature itself, but it cannot be helped. I cannot stop the warmth or fuzziness of my feelings." He went on with describing how he had tried to sleep away his feelings for her, but in all his usual activities, even pouncing, his mind was only on her and her brown eyes, chubby feet, and blasé expression.

His confidence of her acceptance, his assurance of her docility, and his certainty of getting what he wanted tested her excellent training and obedience too far. Her stubbornness came out as the hair on her back raised and her teeth began to show. She responded at last, "You seem to believe that my faithful and affectionate disposition, even more so than my kin, will cause me to roll over and lay down at your offer. I will not. I am positive the unnaturalness of your feelings, as you have described them, will ensure that this is a short-lived game for you and you can be back to your usual amusements very quickly."

Mr. Tabby, who was sitting on the mantelpiece, at first stared silently at her. The M on his forehead became more pronounced as he struggled to comprehend her unforeseen response. He licked his paw and flicked his tail as he said, "And this is your response after all the occasions of your trying to entice me by moving your tail slightly under furniture and rolling on your back in the grass. Now I see the training you have had. I did think that the faithfulness and affection of your reported disposition would indeed cause you to jump heartily at my proposal. I clearly see that my assumptions were flawed. I am most astonished at the manner of your refusal."

"You have expressed the objections you have had to my situation in a most insulting way. You chose to tell me your feelings were against your personality, to the mortification of your family, even counter to your own species! Is that not some cause for incivility, if I was uncivil?" replied she.

"Do you expect me to easily lower myself to your pack's lack of breeding, submission, or lifestyle? One of your sisters is not even fully housebroken! I am not ashamed of the feelings I related. They were not natural but were just, cozy, and fervent. Perhaps the coolness of my manner in hiding my sentiments was the greatest insult to you. Had I lost my usual snooty haughtiness and acted in a tail-wagging, flattering sort of way, you might have a different response right now. But concealment of my feelings with aloof and dignified conduct was the greatest of evil in your opinion."

"You are mistaken, Mr. Tabby, if you suppose the mode of your behaviour has affected me in any way other than that it spared me the concern I might have felt in refusing you had you behaved in a more canine-like manner."

With that Mr. Tabby slowly got up and, not wanting to show any of the shame he felt, stretched slowly and thoroughly in his supercilious manner, nudged a vase off the mantel, and walked out.

DID YOU KNOW?

The Reverend George Austen was a warm, loving father who did all he could to see not only that his ambitious boys succeeded in their professions but also that his brilliant daughter found an audience for her writing beyond the lucky and appreciative family members who acted as her sounding board. This is even more impressive when you realize that it was long before the age of women's liberation.

Moreover, Reverend Austen might have been excused for thinking that much of Jane's violent, vice-filled juvenilia was not exactly suitable material for a respectable clergyman's daughter to be dealing in. Yet he indulged and encouraged her as a child, buying her notebooks and letting her scribble in the parish register the names of imaginary future suitors. In one of the notebooks he gave her, he wrote these sweet words: "Effusions of Fancy by a very Young Lady Consisting of Tales in a Style entirely new." And we've seen how he later wrote to a publisher about *Pride and Prejudice*, even offering to put up his own money to see his daughter's book published.

Mr. Austen was a great reader (as well as a writer of sermons) and read aloud to his children from his vast library. He let them look through his microscope, which no doubt delighted them. He let them put on plays in his barn. Altogether, the parsonage over which Mr. Austen presided must have been a good place for a child to grow up in.

⌐ Pluck and Plumage ⌐
TRACY MARCHINI

As was to be expected, the day that Mallard Bingley arrived at the pond was a blustery one indeed. It was not, however, the wind blowing hot air so much as the beak of Mrs. Bennet.

"Mr. Bennet," she quacked, "I insist that you escort our darling ducklings across the pond immediately. For it's clear that Mallard Bingley has the ability to take up much of the pond, and we'd certainly want our girls to be friendly with such a duck as that. Look at our dear Quane. She and he would make quite the pair indeed."

Mr. Bennet ruffled his feathers, brushed off a few mites, and sat on yesterday's copy of the *Times*. "If you insist, but I think our Quelizabeth is just as good a match as Quane. Not that we play favorites here, of course."

"Please, Mr. Bennet. My nerves. I shall start quacking about my nerves if you don't get off that paper and swim over there. You know how *my* nerves can get on *your* nerves."

"Quite right, dear. Quite right," Mr. Bennet said as he hopped into the pond and started swimming toward the slightly foppish figure of Mallard Bingley. He turned toward his ducklings only once and, for a brief moment, wished they were already flying south for the winter.

Nothing is worse than a pair of young ducklings making a last-minute attempt before the pond freezes, he thought. *It's how I ended up with Mrs. Bennet. She had a shinier beak then, and a quieter one.*

Mallard Bingley waded back and forth, waiting for Mr. Bennet to formally introduce himself. Mr. Bennet did, and Bingley dipped his head in a low bow, bringing up an offering of lake moss. *Quite the gentleman*, Mr. Bennet thought as he devoured the treat.

"Sir," started Mallard Bingley. "I dare say that your lovely ducklings are among the most becoming on the pond. It would be an honor to invite you and your ladies to a wading ball this coming Saturday. I have some friends flying in from out of town, and I am sure that your ladies would be quite the welcome sight to them as well."

Mallard Bingley spread his wings and showed his under-feathers in a gesture of friendship. He was becoming quite agreeable to Mr. Bennet, who thought that perhaps one less duckling to worry about on the flight south would not be such a terrible circumstance after all. He could part with Quane; she wasn't that interesting to talk to anyway. Or perhaps Bingley might take Quydia; she could be quite the handful during a long flight.

Anyway, thought Mr. Bennet, *the ducklings could certainly do worse than this overappeasing mallard.*

Mr. Bennet quacked a goodbye and promised to escort his ducklings of marriageable age across the cooling pond on Saturday.

Upon his return to the Longbourn side of the pond, Mrs. Bennet, Quydia, and Quitty immediately flocked upon him. A plethora of quacks filled the air, and Quane and Quelizabeth would have turned quite red in embarrassment, had their feathers the ability to turn colors. Quary, however, never turned her beak from her Bible and secretly prayed that all of her sisters would go off with the mallard and his friends. It was unnatural the way her sister ducks wanted to dance and take tea together.

Simply unnatural, she thought as she burrowed further into Genesis.

"Well, Quelizabeth," said Mr. Bennet when the quacking had died down. "I pray that you find the mallard agreeable, but I hope indeed that you shouldn't leave me for him. Your mother has it in mind to push Quane on him. I think she'd be agreeable to it; he's got too much sense to take Quydia or Quitty."

Did You Know?

Jane's nephew, James-Edward Austen-Leigh, wrote this now-famous description of his aunt's habits of composition at Chawton:

She had no separate study to retire to, and most of the work must have been done in the general sitting-room, subject to all kinds of casual interruptions. She was careful that her occupation should not be suspected by servants, or visitors, or any persons beyond her own family party. She wrote upon small sheets of paper which could easily be put away, or covered with a piece of blotting paper. There was, between the front door and the offices, a swing door which creaked when it was opened; but she objected to having this little inconvenience remedied, because it gave her notice when anyone was coming.

Quelizabeth looked toward her dear sister Quane, and then across the pond to Mallard Bingley. "He seems rather awkward and dull. I am sure she shall like him very much. For my part, I'll make sure Quane is available for as many dances as possible. I shan't like any of his friends, I'm sure. City ducks are all the same."

"Quite right," Mr. Bennet said. "Quite right. No city ducks for you indeed, my Quizzy."

⤳ Pride, Prejudice, and Revenge ⤳
WESLEY SILER

It is most fitting at this day and time that I be writing to you in this, your hour of need, my dearest Fitzwilliam Darcy. How I have missed you! I hope that this letter finds you in good stead, and I can only hope you think of me as pleasantly as I have thought of you. I know that your recent incarceration is much troubling, and I have hope that I will be able to bring you some joy in spite of this as you look upon my writing.

Everyone around me tells me you are of dastardly reputation and that it would thusly be better for me not to think more on you, or your recent transgression, which has unfortunately landed you into jail, but I find that I cannot. For I know there is no heat and very little in the way of clean water and facilities in such places. I wish there was a way to make your time there more pleasurable, until the most unfortunate thing which must come to pass has.

I wonder, what is your cell like? Has anything of interest happened as you have looked through that small window of yours with the vertical iron bars? I know it must be dreadfully dull. I myself have been asked to attend a fancy dress party. And have it on most good authority that everyone who is anyone will be there. Would that you could be there as well . . . if only . . . if only. I remember the night was beautiful, that rich full moon shining like the sun as we had gone out onto the veranda. I loved the way that your hand dwarfed my own and how your warm lips brushed against mine. My breath quickened as you nuzzled your bearded face against my skin. My heart leapt as you brushed your fingers against the silkiness of my gown, and I knew then I needed to be next to you. After all, I was a woman of five and twenty years, far too long for anyone to be without the comforts of adult company.

But you were not to give me any further interest, no matter how much I played with my hair, batted my lashes, nor even when I had gone so far as to "accidentally" brush my hand across your inner thighs. Nothing . . . nothing. . . . It was then, thirty and three nights ago, I paid a visit to the local apothecary and obtained a sleeping draught. You, my sister Catherine, and I then met some nights later in the pub. I slipped the draught into your mead as you were looking over at Catherine and not at me . . . the one that you should have been concentrating on. The draught took hold, and I helped you from the pub and into a waiting carriage under the auspices of getting you abed and driving us back home.

DID YOU KNOW?

We don't know how many copies of *Sense and Sensibility* were printed—750 or 1,000—but the first edition had sold out by July of 1813. Jane Austen had made a profit of 140, and the few reviews in the press were good. Also good were word-of-mouth reviews: It was discussed at gatherings in high society, and people raved about it in letters to family and friends. Even the royal family was impressed. Fifteen-year-old Princess Charlotte wrote, "I have *just finished* reading; it certainly is interesting, & you feel quite one of the company. I think Maryanne & me are very like in *disposition*, that certainly I am not so good, the same imprudence, &c, however remain very like. I must say it interested me much."

Now, after so many years and so many trials, Jane Austen was seeing her first "child" in print and what's more, she was learning that people were buying it, and reading it, and finding it interested them much.

It was then that I ripped my own clothes and kicked my knickers off, unbuttoning your breeches as well. When my scream echoed throughout the night, and everyone came rushing to my aid, the draught was then starting to wear off and you were only slightly aware of your faculties. With my histrionics, it was all the easier to make people think that you had done the deed that I myself had contrived. I am thereby sending you a little memento along with this letter, my soiled knickers so that you might enjoy them in the moments before the morrow's hanging.

Sincerely yours, Elizabeth Bennet.

⌒ Emma Interrupted ⌒
JOCELYN ARCHER

Emma Housewood, greedy, crafty, and far too wealthy for her own good, was blessed with a somewhat-less-than-sour disposition and the possession of an estate, which many somewhat-better-than-lesser men would happily marry for and united in her form the many blessings of the slightly more than mediocre.

The youngest of nineteen daughters of a most doting and liberal father, Emma had little but that of her own making to ever distress, vex, or otherwise frustrate her. Her mother had died at a young age, mainly of exhaustion, and so Emma kept house for her father once her sisters had married suitable young men of the most noble professions with handsome estates of their own, or at least so was Emma's impression, though she retained little memory of those things which pertained to beings other than herself.

As her mother was dead, Emma herself had been raised by the most kind of governesses, a woman whose laziness and love of distraction never allowed her to show Emma unkindness in the form of harsh words or deeds. The two were more like sisters than teacher and pupil, or so they were considered, mainly due to the fact that Emma's rich diet caused slight pockmarks and a less-than-delicate figure which gave her an air of one twice her own age.

When her governess married, Emma was not sure how she could bear the loss. What would she do without another being in the house entirely lacking in any desire to better or edify Emma? How could she live without a friend to verify her own high opinions of herself and low opinions of others? No one but Emma herself could ever esteem her as Miss Tyler had. Sadly, Emma accepted the fact that her one true friend and sister would be the great distance of one hour's carriage ride away and set upon a most important task, to find one closer whom she could impart her wisdom on and whose will was easier to bend to her own. By luck, the very next day she met the toady and obsequious Hester Merwin, and her newest of projects began.

⟶ Wild and Wanton Jane ⟵
ANABELLA BLOOM

After a day spent in professions of love and schemes of felicity, Mr. Collins worked up the courage to kiss his fiancée. He had been thinking of it most earnestly since their private walk. Preparing her for this advance in their relationship, he felt, was his solemn duty, and therefore he spent several minutes lecturing on the state of an engagement and how it was very like a marriage in the eyes of all, especially with steady characters such as theirs. Then, proceeding to wet his mouth as to not make the experience unpleasant, he took her by the arms and pressed his mouth to hers.

Charlotte was by no means deficient in knowledge when it came to such matters. She had grown up on a farm, tending to animals, and had a fair bit of knowledge of husbandry. Though she did not suppose humans mated like sheep, she understood well how a child was conceived. And her mother, wishing to help her advance her engagement before the joyous event took place, had been obliged to suggest helpful hints into securing Mr. Collins's interest.

Though Charlotte hardly doubted Mr. Collins's intent, she knew one word from Lady Catherine, whom she had never met, would be sufficient in turning his regard and making him end the engagement before the wedding took place. Only a strong inducement on her part would secure her lot, and she intended to see that her future was indeed hers. So it was, as Mr. Collins pressed his lips to hers on the private bench, she allowed her hand to slide onto his thigh, as if by unconscious design, and pretended to be so enraptured by his kiss that she did not know what she did. Her fingers kneaded into his leg, indecently high, and she felt the muscles stiffen beneath her hand.

Mr. Collins instantly took hold of her face, pressing most earnestly against her so that her teeth cut into the tender flesh of her mouth. There was no art to his lovemaking, for the indelicate fumblings of his hands were hardly adept for the task. However, this did not stop him from taking control of the situation, and so he took Charlotte's hand and moved it up to caress the heavy press of his manhood through his breeches. The sensation was all too pleasurable, and he began to rock most insistently.

Trembling and sighing in great turn, he released her mouth and quickly undid his breeches so that flesh might meet flesh. He felt no qualms in using his fiancée in such a way, for he had given the matter a great deal of thought in the time they were parted and determined that should such an occasion arise, he was well within his rights to take advantage of it. He led her hand to his shaft and noted with great appreciation her look of modesty as she turned her eyes away from him. Applying pressure, he showed her how he wished for her to move.

To Charlotte, she thought of the task not unlike milking a cow. Though such thoughts were not those of a proper bride-to-be, she could not help them. She looked upon sex as another chore that must be performed. Mr. Collins was quite content to let her stroke him as he buried his face into her chest and played with her breasts through the barrier of her gown. He made strange noises, breathing hard and fast, until finally she milked him of his seed. Afterward, she was pleasantly surprised to find him so grateful for the service that he hardly said anything at all and they were obliged to pass several hours in silence.

DID YOU KNOW?

It is a truth universally acknowledged that the first line of *Pride and Prejudice* is the best and most famous opening sentence in English literature and the gateway to one of the world's greatest pleasures. So it is surprising to see the mild praise of the novel that appears in reviews written at the time it was first published. These reviews were favorable, as they had been in response to *Sense and Sensibility*, but they focused approvingly on the book's morality and barely seemed to notice its breathtaking wit! However, there was a difference in tone between published reviews of *Pride and Prejudice* and social gossip about it, and the latter was much more interesting and spirited.

The first edition of 1,500 copies had sold out by July of 1813. A second edition was published that fall, and a third would be published in 1817. It was *the* novel to read or, as Anne Isabella Milbanke (who would later marry Lord Byron) put it, it was "at present the fashionable novel." Maria Edgeworth, whom Jane admired, read it and urged her brother in a letter to do so also. Warren Hastings praised it, to Jane's delight. The playwright Richard Sheridan said *Pride and Prejudice* "was one of the cleverest things" he had ever read. The high praise from prominent writers must have been especially gratifying to Austen.

Pride and Prejudice was published anonymously, which was how Jane liked it. As a result, however, many people had the wrong woman down as the author—and others thought it too good to have been written by a woman at all. Henry Austen, though sworn to secrecy like the rest of those in the know, let slip the secret of Jane's authorship more than once. Jane forgave him since his motivation was rooted in "Brotherly vanity and Love"—and of course because it was Henry—but she appreciated the superior discretion of her brother Frank and his wife.

From poor Miss Benn to the highest members of high society, Elizabeth Bennet was working her charm while her creator watched and listened with amusement and satisfaction.

PART 2

If Jane Could See Us Now

A number of the entries we received in the Bad Austen contest were set in contemporary times. The juxtaposition of Austen's nineteenth-century sensibility with the realities of the twenty-first century created a fair amount of amusement on the part of the editors, who did a lot of chortling—and hope you will, too. Herewith, stories that Jane Austen never wrote but quite possibly would have, if she'd lived a few centuries later.

⤳ Pemberley High ⤳
R. STANDFORD

It is universally acknowledged that high school is a form of medieval torture invented by embittered adults to retaliate against the inconvenience youth has caused them. This was never more true than for an outspoken, sharp-witted junior named Lizzi. Her unconventional dress and various charitable causes, including most recently "What Are Men Compared to Mountains: A Weekend of Womanhood and Nature Retreat," earned her much notability and scorn amongst the jocks and cheerleaders that roamed the halls of Pemberley High.

Today was no different, though as Lizzi ran to her locker and hastily pulled out her science book, she noticed a lack of mockery. *Perhaps they have finally seen the wisdom of my nature.*

Then, she noticed that the halls, normally full of hormonal animals, referred to as students, engaging in mating and social rituals which Lizzi felt were unnecessary and demeaning to an individual, were empty, save her.

She glanced down at her watch.

"Shoot," Lizzi said. Late again. It was so easy for her mind to wander during her walk to school, and Lizzi often found herself lost in contemplation over a wayward daisy or rose that lay on her path to school. Sighing, she was about to renounce herself to the dull dribble called chemistry when a splash of color invaded her vision.

"Hey," she said, turning.

A boy, well-dressed in a polo and dark jeans, handsome with a brooding stare, stood in front of her, nervously clutching a piece of paper.

"Are you new? Lost?" Lizzi said. "I can show you where your classes are."

"...I..."

"Let me help." Lizzi reached for the paper.

The young gentlemen recoiled as her hand brushed against his.

"Don't pay her any heed," Caroline said, appearing from the shadows.

She was dressed immaculately, every accessory matching her cheerleading captain outfit, which she wore every day. This monotony made Lizzi's stomach churn.

"I fear I might be ill," Lizzi said under her breath.

"I'll show you around and protect you from the pariahs that infest the hallways." Caroline batted her eyelashes and interlaced her arm with the stranger.

He smirked at Lizzi, to acknowledge his awareness and acceptance of his and her social standing, and, Lizzi suspected, to rub her face in that knowledge.

"Of all the arrogant fools!" Lizzi exclaimed. "See if I ever help him."

Lizzi had all but forgotten the incident by the time she arrived at chemistry class and was entirely ready to immerse herself in the world of formulas and equations when an all-too-familiar face appeared at the door.

"Class," the teacher said, "we have a new student. Meet Mr. Darcy. I assume you will all reveal your charitable nature to him in time."

Did You Know?

Thomas Egerton published *Mansfield Park*, as he had *Sense and Sensibility* and *Pride and Prejudice*, but either he knew it was not the crowd pleaser that *Pride and Prejudice* was and offered to publish it only on commission or he offered an unacceptably low price for the copyright. In either case, this novel was published on commission also. The first edition of probably 1,250 copies was published in May of 1814 and sold out within six months, so it was surprising and disappointing when Egerton declined to publish a second edition. His instincts were right: When Henry negotiated with a different publisher to bring out a second edition in 1816—also on commission—it did not sell and was remaindered the following year. Perhaps Austen's own comment that this novel was "not half so entertaining" as *Pride and Prejudice* expressed the common view.

To Jane's disappointment, there were no contemporary reviews of *Mansfield Park*. (Serious authors whose work is ignored by the press today can perhaps take some comfort in that fact.) We do, however, have a fascinating document containing responses to the novel: Jane herself recorded the opinions of *Mansfield Park* expressed by family, friends, neighbors, and other acquaintances. One opinion that does indeed show up repeatedly is that it is not as good as *Pride and Prejudice*. Frank Austen and his wife, Mary, felt this way; so did Edward and his sons Edward and George; Mrs. Austen; Charles; and Jane's friend, the Godmersham governess, Anne Sharp.

Anna, Jane's intelligent, spirited niece, "could not bear Fanny." The strength of her disgust comes through loud and clear! And Mrs. Austen, no slouch in the intelligence department herself, "thought Fanny insipid"—as many readers have thought since. It is interesting to see that while many readers—particularly since around the middle of the twentieth century—have in fact found *Mansfield Park* the most interesting, sophisticated, and complex of Austen's novels, and certainly the most difficult to "figure out," the general opinion is no doubt the same that was heard by Jane— *Pride and Prejudice* is preferred. And, as members of her own family did at the time of the book's publication, many readers continue to dislike the heroine Fanny—and the hero Edmund, for that matter—and much prefer the morally corrupt but very entertaining figures of Mary and Henry Crawford.

"He's very easy on the eyes," a perky blonde chirped.

"If you like the conceited type." Lizzi's laugh echoed to the corners of the classroom.

"And I hear his parents bought the mansion that had been left to dust on the corner of Main," said the blonde.

"One thing in his favor, I suppose," Lizzi replied. "Though even if he had all the money in the world, that would not make up for his lack of manners."

"What was that, Miss Bennet?" her teacher replied.

"I was just welcoming the fine and honorable Mr. Darcy to Pemberley High," Lizzi said, standing. "We had the pleasure of meeting earlier today. I am sure with his disposition, he'll have no trouble making friends."

Though no one else seemed to notice, Lizzi thought she perceived a slight discoloration in the new student's cheeks.

"How very kind of you," her teacher replied. "And since you were the first to show our school's 'welcoming spirit,' I'm sure you'll have no problem honoring Mr. Darcy by being his lab partner. Kid, go take a seat next to our self-appointed welcoming committee."

"I'd be honored to be his partner," the blonde said.

The teacher replied that she already had a perfectly good lab partner.

"Sir," Lizzi retorted, "you and I had an arrangement regarding partnerships—"

"Yes. Yes, you're independent and don't need a partner because it's 'demeaning' to your self-esteem and sense of womanhood," the teacher replied. "But Mr. Darcy is in want of a lab partner, and as you are, by your own actions, the only student without a partner, there seems to be only one solution to our problems."

Lizzi shrunk down into her seat as the boy sat next to her.

"I ... er ... Hi," he whispered. "This morning—I can explain—you see, some of us are not as endowed—"

"Spare me your excuses," Lizzi hissed. "Let's just figure out a way to make it through the semester."

⤳ Regency Matchmaking ⤳
STACEY GRAHAM

"Welcome, welcome, one and all to Regency Matchmaking! I am your hostess, Mrs. Bennet, the mother of five daughters—three of which have made excellent matches due to my influence—and two whom I will no doubt be finding suitable husbands for this afternoon. Shall we get started?"

Mrs. Bennet snapped the card with her fingers, signaling her daughters Mary and Kitty to be seated. The screen separating the girls from their mother stretched nearly the length of the television studio, masking the girls' expression of horror at their mother's interference in their love lives.

"I beseech you to hold, Mrs. Bennet." Her voice rising from backstage, Caroline Bingley emerged from the shadows while signaling a footman to bring a chair and place it next to Kitty. "You may now continue. I fear I am in need of your skills, Madam, though we will never speak of this publicly again." Adjusting her shawl to cover her bony shoulders, she ignored the young women, staring instead at the smattering of people making up the studio audience.

"Er, yes, of course, Miss Bingley. I'm pleased you are down from London to join us." Her head rapidly cocking to the side, Mrs. Bennet signaled her husband to block any further female intruders from the stage. Her daughters needed no further competition.

"Our first suitor hails from Northanger Abbey. He's handsome, clever, and a bit of a charmer. Ladies, please give a Longbourn welcome to Captain Frederick Tilney."

A smidgen of polite applause filled the studio as Captain Tilney strode onto the stage, bowing slightly to Mrs. Bennet and throwing a wink to her husband. Scowling at this foolishness, Mr. Bennet returned to his book.

Once Captain Tilney was seated in the Bennets' best chair, she began. "Sir, am I correct in my information that you are heir to a rather large establishment?"

Miss Bingley defied her perfect posture by leaning slightly forward in her seat to catch his answer. She was not disappointed by the strong timbre of his voice nor his succinct response.

"Yes, Madam. Northanger Abbey will be mine at the passing of the General, though it now stands bereft of a woman's touch and I will need a wife to manage the estate once I assume rightful ownership."

"Very good, Captain Tilney. I have no doubt either of my daughters," a long cough erupting from behind the screen interrupted Mrs. Bennet's declaration, "and Miss Bingley, of course, would suit you perfectly."

"Captain Tilney," Caroline interrupted, "can you tell me more what you are looking for in a wife? I so tire of men wanting only a quick roll in the stables without noticing my excellence in station, my accomplishments, my . . . FINE EYES." Irritation scorched her words, the sting of being thrown over for the niece of a man who resides in Cheapside scraped at her pride. The irony of sitting with that woman's sisters competing for a man was not lost on her, though desperate times called for desperate measures. She was nearly an old maid and would need to secure a husband quite soon.

"As you wish, Madam. I search for a woman of fortune and candor—and one who doesn't mind a scoundrel." A smile slid across his face as he heard the ladies draw in a quick breath at his admission of being a rapscallion.

"Finally!" Caroline Bingley sprung from her chair with more vigor than either Kitty or Mary had seen from the older woman. Crossing the barrier, Caroline stood before Tilney. "You had me at 'large establishment.'"

"I believe we have an understanding, Miss Bingley?"

She nodded, taking in the breadth of his shoulders and the fit of his waistcoat as he stood. He would do nicely; she was certain she could tame his wickedness to become a proper husband. Then again, a bit of a rogue never hurt anyone.

"Well, I have never been so affronted! And in my own studio, too!" Mrs. Bennet was flustered. Her plans for the afternoon partially ruined by the upstart, Miss Bingley, she ushered the new couple quickly offstage, then returned to her station.

"Kitty! Mary! Sit still, girls. We have another gentleman of good breeding. May I introduce Mr. Willoughby of Combe Magna...."

⌒ Through Kitties' Eyes ⌒
MARGARET K. GATES

"Megan, I think Alfred has noticed me," said Rosanne. "We passed twice in the halls today, and he smiled both times."

"I saw him staring at you from across the cafeteria," said her sister.

The two cats sitting at the opposite end of the parlor stood up. Cinnamon, the black-and-white one, spoke. "Which girl do you choose, Orchid?"

The yellow cat licked her paw as she pondered the matter, then said, "Rosanne's wearing black, and Megan has light blue slacks. I'll shed my fur on Rosanne, and your black fur will stand out against Megan's blue clothing."

"Great choice. Let's go."

The cats sauntered to the sofa and settled in the girls' laps.

"Alfred dumped Susie last week." Rosanne stroked Orchid's back as she spoke.

Orchid interpreted the words to Cinnamon. "Sir Alfred has realized Susie's unworthiness and wonders how he could have overlooked the charms of Lady Rosanne who is obviously an elegant female."

"He'd be a good catch; he's the star basketball player," said Megan.

Cinnamon responded, "He's also tall, of comely appearance, and his family has an abundance of shekels. I could continue this panegyric."

"His sister spoke to me after class today; she never had before."

"Sir Alfred commissioned a spy to scrutinize Lady Rosanne's personality."

"Aren't you glad you didn't repeat to anyone what you thought of her new hairstyle?"

"How fortunate that your unparalleled elegance precluded a repetition of your communication to me describing the rat's nest on Sir Alfred's sister's head." Cinnamon rubbed a paw against her own head for emphasis.

"I plan to compliment her to her best friend," said Rosanne. "She's a nice enough girl, really."

"A well-spoken word of approbation will reach her brother's ears and endear me to him."

"Maybe he'll ask you to the school dance next week."

Cinnamon continued to mimic Megan's words. "A ball is an inimitable location in which to secure a gentleman's affections. Consider Cinderella."

"Oh, wouldn't that be cool! I'm the best dancer in my grade."

"Oh, what delight, what felicity!" Orchid rolled onto her back, pointed her paws toward the four corners of the parlor, and sighed.

"Yes, humans are ridiculous," said Cinnamon, "but they feed us and provide a warm home safe from dogs. And how their follies amuse us."

Rosanne spoke again. "But what if he asks Carolyn instead? She's had her eye on Alfred for a month. I'd be sick if she got him."

"But what despair would flood my soul should Sir Alfred deign to favor the base Carolyn with his attentions. She must be totally profligate to try to steal him from me."

"Such a thought turns my stomach," said her sister. "I never did like her."

"If she purloins him away, I'll have an enjoyment of original dislikes. But Orchid, let's beat it before our fervid emotion constrains us to swoon alternately on the sofa."

DID YOU KNOW?

Jane Austen had just one sister, Cassandra, who, although older than Jane, would survive her. Her sisters-in-law were another story, and Jane watched as, one after another, the wives of her brothers met an early death.

The eldest Austen son, James, married Anne Mathew, who was a little older than he was. Anne gave birth to Jane Anna Elizabeth, known as Anna, in April of 1793. Almost exactly two years later, Anne died suddenly at home. The doctor diagnosed it as probably a ruptured liver. Anne Austen was in her mid-thirties when she died. Edward Austen's wife, Elizabeth, died at the age of thirty-five after giving birth to her eleventh child. Pretty and elegant Elizabeth, the daughter of a Kentish baronet, had married at eighteen and spent the remaining years of her life as a devoted wife and mother.

Then there was Henry's wife, Eliza, with whom Jane was very close. Eliza died at the age of fifty-one, probably of breast cancer. According to the account of Jane and Henry both, Eliza endured a long, painful illness before dying in the spring of 1813.

The baby of the family, Charles Austen, married seventeen-year-old Fanny Palmer in Bermuda while he was serving in the Royal Navy. Fanny bore Charles three daughters and then died after giving birth to a fourth girl. The baby died a few weeks later. Fanny Austen was only twenty-four years old.

⌁ Sense & Circuitry: Cyberth 1813 ⌁
MARGARET FISKE

It is a truth gone viral that a bachelor, possessing disposable fortune, is in want of a gadget. Thus, Manly Doolittle, both eligible and old-moneyed from the dot-com boom, parlayed an afternoon of lucrative roulette into a trip to Squire Eddy's Cut-Rate Electronics Emporium, where he impulse-purchased the Cybertha 1813, Automaton of Menial Drudgery for the Chore-Impaired.

"Mightier than five crack-head liverymen," the box promised. He galloped her home to Slackersborough Park to assemble her forthwith.

From the first moment her sensors identified him as a dashing man, and not a giant dachshund, she regarded her master in the

highest esteem. He slammed the battery hatch shut on her der-
riere with gusto.

"Madame, you will now commence to scour this residence
from rug to rafter. Guests are due in an hour, so concoct some
snackage aforehand."

The hour passed in a blur of brush over broom. At the stroke
of nine sharp, a horde descended on Slackersborough, one and
all ardently typing, texting, or tweeting, with thumbs vigorously
a-twiddle. Each guest solely focused on his or her own companion in a box.

Master Doolittle welcomed them heartily. "Allow my mecha-
nized charwoman to trade your cloaks for libations." The flesh
maidens momentarily paused activity to glare. Their snarky comments dripped with venom. "Swiffer! Chrysler! Ho-bot!" they
sniffed, then they resumed fiddling with their gizmos. The gentlemen perused ribald portraitures on their Blackberries and would
not have noticed Armageddon.

The evening dragged its leaden feet like a spoilt child avoid-
ing bedtime. Cybertha rapidly resented the constant fetchings
of Liquid Panty Remover and Chicken Fingers Marengo for
such boors. They persisted to suck up the suds in uncouth silence
occasionally pierced by a ringtone. Defriending lots, befriending
naught, offering zero face time to visages already present at the
party.

Suddenly, Absinthea Pollick waved a hanky in her face. "Yoo-
hoo! Cleaning thingy! Lady Ditzchild has laid her lunch upon

the drapery. Attend it posthaste, before more luncheons are likewise divulged."

With each angry mop-stroke, the 1813's antislight protocol plotted a vengeance program.

Finding the bidet occupied, Cybertha rolled to the balcony to cast down the drape water. There she found Lady Ditzchild perched atop the balustrade rail seeking better iPod reception. "Look! Abandoned Blahniks!" Cybertha exclaimed.

"Guh?" said Lady Ditzchild, whose vocal chords had atrophied from disuse. She squinted at the abyss. Iron claws unexpectedly shoved the drunkenette forcibly on the buttocks. Milady's sparse diet of opium and Jägerbombs rendered her weak as beige rouge. She splashed into River Wettyford and vanished in a flash of bling.

The Blahnik ruse succeeded swimmingly. Soon all the ladies were dispatched to the river bobbing for shoes. Nobody noticed their absence. They did, however, notice the booze was gone.

Potables parched, the gentlemen bid adieu and ventured for the public house to continue celebrating. Regrettably, the driver, Lumpfellow, was overly engrossed Skyping fallen angels in Rome when he disregarded the bridge and steered the chaise and V6 into the Wettyford. "BRB," IMed Idleman, but sadly they were not. Days later, seven bloated corpses would wash ashore at Shirkershire, still clutching their handhelds and cocktails.

Erstwhile, back at the manor, a new scheme was brewing. Spent from merriment and a dozen Milk of Amnesia shooters, Master lost consciousness on the divan. Cybertha gazed upon his snoring personage, full of Happy Valentines notions. While he dozed, the 1813 emotional simulator surfed the dream sea of romantic delusion. Doolittle had the hazelest eyeballs, the winsomest spinal pelt. Those wooly muttonchops absolutely ewe-jitsued her heart wires. She yearned to caress every pixel of his body; to rip the very music of his soul and burn it into her memory as a playlist entitled "Master Jams," then to listen to it again and again and again whilst he downloaded upon her. Her motherboard began to deliciously overheat.

Perhaps it was the incandescent twinkle from her vision sockets or the thrum of her twirling libido that awoke Doolittle. He arose in intense vexation. "What in the deuce are you gawking at? Wretched wrench wench! You freak me out verily!" Swiftly, he bonneted her with someone's soiled delicates. 'Twas more than any mechanical chambermaid could possibly bear.

For a fortmoment, she discarded etiquette and gave her beloved a sound drubbing with the fondue pot. Master Doolittle appeared expired. All the sense ran out of his head, and he ceased to be amusing. She thought about frilly petticoats to masque the carnage until her circuitry compelled her to tidy the crime scene.

While rummaging in the garage for a burial shroud, Cybertha spied the Rug Doctor, standing buff and impeccable, alone in the corner. She fell head over wheels smitten. A physician! With gynecological knowledge! Quite a fortuitous match indeed!

Did You Know?

From her earliest writings, Jane Austen mocked the convention that a novel's heroine had to be perfect. No Bridget Joneses for the eighteenth-century novel-reading crowd! In *Love and Freindship*, the heroine Laura describes herself: "Lovely as I was, the Graces of my Person were the least of my Perfections. Of every accomplishment accustomary to my sex, I was Mistress. . . . In my Mind, every Virtue that could adorn it was centered; it was the Rendezvous of every good Quality and of every noble sentiment." In the "Plan of a Novel" inspired by suggestions from Mr. Clarke, the heroine is a "faultless Character herself."

"Perfection" was a condition that could only be made entertaining to Austen by mockery of it, hence the great number of absurdly idealized heroines in the juvenilia. But in a letter to her niece Fanny, Austen states straightforwardly what she shows ironically: "Pictures of perfection as you know make me sick & wicked."

⌒ Fools and Folly ⌒
SUSAN G. MANZI

Cassandra handed Jane her coffee saying, "Here is your skinny mocha latte, no whip, one Splenda. I could not resist getting a brownie for each of us, too; do they not look delicious?" She sat down next to her sister.

"Pray, how much more time do we have before this signing starts?" Jane asked.

"I believe we have about five minutes. Jane, can you guess who is first in line?"

"Oh, please, do not tell me he has come to yet another signing. I do not think I can bear it." Jane put her hand to her head. "I think I am getting a slight headache. Maybe we should cancel, Cassandra."

"Too late. Here he comes, Jane. Take a deep breath and all will be well."

"Hello, your Royal Highness. How good of you to come. But I do believe I have already signed your copy of *Emma*, your Royal Highness."

"Yes, yes, you are quite right, but this is my copy of *Sense and Sensibility*. And look." He opened his book. "No signature!"

"You are quite right, your Royal Highness. I shall sign it at once," Jane answered, smiling with clenched teeth, trying not to divulge the revulsion she felt when looking at him.

An unpleasant thought flashed in Cassandra's head, a scene where she is delivering coffee to Jane, who now lives in the Tower of London. Cassandra casually squeezed Jane's leg to remind her sister to control herself.

Jane took a deep breath, looking toward her sister and then to the Prince Regent.

"Do you have any specific requests, your Royal Highness, in regards to the inscription to be written in this book?" Jane put a wry smile on. "I have no other novels to dedicate to you, I fear, so this will have to suffice today."

"Miss Austen, you may decide what to write. After all, you are the writer."

Jane pondered for a moment what to write. Maybe she would pick up her quill one last time and write what she really thought of the blundering fool. Jane collected her thoughts, took a deep breath, and began writing.

To His Royal Highness, The Prince Regent, I am humbled by your continual attentions to my works and wish to tell you that if there are any other books you would like me to sign, you are welcome to send a servant, there is no need for HRH to take such risks with his health. Your obedient servant, Jane Austen.

The Prince picked up his book, read the entry, then looked at Miss Austen, wondering why on earth she would not want him to continue attending her book signings. The Prince bowed, still unsure what to make of the comment written in his book, and took his leave.

Cassandra and Jane burst into laughter when he exited the store.

"Oh Jane, you do taunt that man so dreadfully!"

Jane smiled, then signaled to the next person in line that she was ready.

"Hello, Miss Austen, I have just finished reading a book for the first time. It was your *Sense and Sensibility*. It was hard to understand since you wrote it in, like, a strange type of language. Luckily, I found out that all your books have been made into movies, so I put them on my Netflix queue."

"Oh, I see. Pray tell what is your name?"

"Lindsay, with an A. The press is always writing my name with an E and it drives me crazy."

"Then you are someone of fame. May I ask what is your surname?"

"Lohan, Lindsay Lohan. I have had a lot of extra time on my hands recently, so I decided to try and read a book for a change."

Jane smiled, took her pen, and wrote.

Lindsay—Thank you for reading S&S, how nice it is that my book found its way into your nicotine-stained hands. I do hope that you have actually paid for this book. I encourage you to read another book while you are incarcerated; it shall help make the time go by much more quickly while living in a cell. With all the sincerity I can feel for you, Jane Austen.

"Yes, who's next?"

Did You Know?

The year 1811, when Austen started writing *Mansfield Park*, was the year that George, Prince of Wales, was appointed prince-regent. His father, King George III, was insane and therefore incompetent to rule. The prince-regent threw himself an enormously expensive and lavish party to celebrate, which the nation certainly could not afford but which was right in keeping with the general behavior of the decadent, fashionable, and immoral princes. Vice and scandal tainted the royal household, with adultery and gambling just some of the popular activities among its members.

Whether or not Austen subtly worked her opinion of the prince-regent into *Mansfield Park*, she stated it flatly in a letter in response to the public battles of the regent and his wife, in which the prince accused the princess of adultery, and she now defended herself in a letter to the *Morning Chronicle*. Jane wrote: "I suppose all the World is sitting in Judgement upon the Princess of Wales's letter. Poor Woman, I shall support her as long as I can, because she *is* a Woman, & because I hate her Husband."

So how, then, did *Emma*, Jane's next novel, come to be dedicated to this man?

Henry became ill while he was negotiating with a new publisher, John Murray, founder of the influential *Quarterly Review*, who had agreed to publish *Emma*. One of the doctors who attended him was a court physician who told Jane that the prince was a great admirer of her work, with a set of her novels in each of his residences. Although those novels had been published anonymously, Jane's authorship was no longer a close secret by this time (and probably not one Henry would have kept from his doctors in any case). This doctor also informed the prince that Miss Austen was in town. The result was that the Reverend James Stanier Clarke, the librarian of the regent's lavish and grand Carlton House, visited her at Henry's and then invited her to visit Carlton House in turn. It appears that during this visit Mr. Clarke suggested she might dedicate her next novel to the prince. Although Jane at first hesitated to do so, she soon understood that she had received a command—and her simple dedication was turned into something quite gaudier by Murray.

Sarah and Katherine
LAURA DRAVENSTOTT

The ladies entered the room decorously, proceeding at a modest pace whilst the gentleman indicated the appropriate seats, upon which they were to recline gracefully during the whole of the interview. The first lady, indeed, was all smiles and amiability, nodding to one and to the other as she surveyed the room and took notes of which cameraman might be disposed to present her at the most beneficial angle, and she favored him with a nod, aware that her entrance from the left of the stage presented her figure to great benefit.

The second lady presented a visage more inclined to the sedate, not serious to be sure but yet reluctant to compose such smiles as wreathed the face of her more amiable companion. Indeed, it seemed to the cameraman that she had perhaps much at stake and that her reserve, though modest, indicated a sterner mental faculty than her partner, which perhaps would bode ill for the first lady.

The gentlewomen were seated. The first, the most honorable governor, Mrs. Palin, made certain that her spectacles were aligned most becomingly and demonstrated her prepossession with another smile and nod at the assemblage. The second, the elegant and reserved Mrs. Couric, found her focus not upon the opposite lady's countenance, but upon her hairstyle, which elevation and contrivance seemed most amazing.

Mrs. Couric opened their intercourse with a condescending query as to her companion's experience with foreign nations. "My dear Mrs. Palin, I have heard you state that your proximity—in your fair home of Alaska—to other nations contributes to your experience in the areas of foreign policy with these nations. Would you take the trouble to explain what you have meant by that?"

Mrs. Palin tilted her excellently coiffed head. She reflected but briefly on what she was to include in her response, preferring more to rely upon the goodwill of her companion than to any wit or intelligence that might be required of the answer. "Why, Mrs. Couric, to be sure! I was merely indicating that Alaska—my home state, which you are, of course, acquainted with—has quite a narrow maritime border between itself and a foreign country, which is Russia. On our other side is the land, the boundary you might say, that we have with Canada. I found it rather startling and not so very amusing that my comment was ill treated by the uncouth reporters who rather . . ." She hesitated, confused either of how to reprimand said reporters or of which syllables were most appropriate to include in her pretty speech.

Mrs. Couric courteously rushed to provide a word for her amiable companion. "Did they mock you, my dear Governor Palin?"

"Yes, mocked. I suppose that is the word. Indeed."

Mrs. Couric delicately cleared her throat and proceeded upon this line of questioning, the object of which, though pointed, had yet to reveal any definite danger to the fair respondent. "If you might explain to me why that position— of Alaska—enhances your refinement and credentials in the arena of foreign policy?"

Governor Palin's smile drooped but little as she perceived the less-than-generous vein of her companion's inquiry. "It most certainly does! Of course! Our neighbors—the very neighbors that adjoin to our state in the location next door—they are foreign countries. They are in the fair state that I am currently the executive of. And there, in Russia . . ."

"Have you, yourself, ever had the occasion to be personally involved with any negotiations, for example, with the Russians?"

"Well, we have trade missions back and forth. We—, we do! It's very important when you consider even national security issues with Russia as that rogue and ill-mannered scallywag, Mr. Putin, rears his head and enters the airspace of the fair United States of America—I ask you, where, where do they go? I tell you, good Mrs. Couric, it is Alaska. It is just right over the border. It is from Alaska that we send those out to make sure that an eye is being kept on this very powerful nation, Russia, because they are right there. They are right next to—to our state."

The fair governor had some difficulty in responding and hoped that some change of subject would avail. Mrs. Couric allowed herself to reflect for the briefest moment how the interlude may reflect fairly on her networking career. For in some aspect of her adept mind, she had recognized that this interview would in a fair way encourage the offer—to her—of broadcasting's most honorable prizes. It put her in mind to retain quite a good temper.

DID YOU KNOW?

Although *Persuasion* was Jane Austen's last completed novel, she did leave a fragment of another one. In January of 1817 she began working on a new book, and the last date on the manuscript is March 18, 1817. She died exactly four months later. While *Persuasion* is romantic and contains a good deal of melancholy, *Sanditon* is briskly comic. It is hard to believe it was written while the author's health must have been declining rapidly. Neither the style nor the subject matter betray that fact.

One of the things Austen appears to be satirizing in *Sanditon* is, in sweeping terms, the spirit of change. Innovation and commercialization, the story *seems* to say, are ridiculous and wrong and bad for the country. Yet, although the satire frequently aims at those targets, Austen actually draws a picture in which they appear in a positive light at least as often, and it is not at all clear that she didn't enjoy and welcome such change as much as she mistrusted it.

The Eldest, the Youngest & Matchmaker.com
TAMI ABSI

Elizabeth drew her favorite china teacup from her lips and rested it on the saucer. The delicate plate protected the articles on her drawing table: a quill pen, some ivory stationary, and a computer.

She searched for Matchmaker.com and scrolled through the competition first. The titles before the ladies' names were impressive, but a reader learned little else past the maidens' monikers. The comments posted revealed the ladies to be empty-headed with nothing worth saying. Elizabeth imagined those women received several invitations from equally unimpressive suitors, no less than knights.

Lydia sauntered into the room, hoping to search for the latest fashions, for which Elizabeth showed perfect unconcern. When Lydia saw the screen, she stopped dead and grew pale. "My dear sister, why are you looking at the women?" she said with an indelicate amount of concern. "Surely, you're not indeed." Her voice trailed off, too horrified to speak of it.

Elizabeth hid an impudent grin. "Why, no, not that. I wanted to see with whom I might compete before profiling."

"You haven't profiled? You are almost twenty-one. Do you not fear spinsterhood?" gasped Lydia. "Let me help you. There is no reason to scroll and look at each and every one of them. See? Thus, you order the women by rank, inheritance, numbers of servants, and the orderliness of their homes. With the last category, I suppose the webmasters were want of a rank for the lower-class women with no real basis for breeding."

Elizabeth commandeered the mouse. "The men, my dear Lydia, can they be thus arrayed?"

"Certainly, but with the men, their pictures speak volumes, and only the eye can categorize them to my liking," Lydia stated while smoothing her best, silken gown.

"Ah," Elizabeth sighed. "You are the youngest. Is it proper for you to be cataloging men? Prudence dictates you should be the last to marry."

Lydia pulled powder from her purse and dabbed her forehead. "I could not wait for all four of you, especially at your pace. The light is good this time of the evening, and with a lit candle beside the monitor, you'll take a fine profile picture. Let me show you how to take a romantic-looking portrait."

In the midst of her comments, she pushed up her corset and forced her sleeves a bit farther down her shoulders. Elizabeth could hear stitches popping, and she knew Mother would be annoyed.

After Elizabeth had profiled for the first time and after Lydia updated her picture, Elizabeth shared another concern. She said, "There is so much more about a man than one can assess through these pages."

"How so, sister?" Lydia challenged.

"What of the way he moves, especially on the dance floor? How will he interview me as we stroll across the park to visit the neighbors? Is there no way to line them up according to their love for art, knowledge of music, singing, or, perhaps, tone of voice?"

DID YOU KNOW?

On March 23, 1817, five days after laying aside the manuscript of *Sanditon* for good, Jane Austen wrote to her niece Fanny: "I certainly have not been well for many weeks, & about a week ago I was very poorly, I have had a good deal of fever at times & indifferent nights, but am considerably better now, & recovering my Looks a little, which have been bad enough, black & white & every wrong colour." In addition to fevers and facial discoloration, Austen also suffered from gastrointestinal distress. She often felt weak—sometimes very weak—and one of her early complaints was of back pain. These symptoms grew more and more severe over the next few months, although there were periods in which she rallied.

In May, Jane was taken to Winchester to be treated by doctors there. Although she had good days, her doctor, Mr. Lyford, held out no hope.

On July 17 Cassandra and Mary Austen, James's wife, saw Jane's condition change. Mr. Lyford pronounced her close to death, saying a large blood vessel had burst, and gave her laudanum to ease her suffering. Cassandra asked her if she wanted anything, and she replied, "Nothing but death." She lost consciousness and at half past four in the morning, with her head on a pillow in Cassandra's lap, she died. Jane Austen was forty-one years old.

In a 1964 article in the *British Medical Journal*, Sir Zachary Cope diagnosed Austen's fatal illness, based on the record of her symptoms, as Addison's disease, a tuberculosis of the adrenal glands. A letter in response to this by F.A. Bevan suggests that a lymphoma such as Hodgkin's disease was the likelier cause of her death. There is continued debate and speculation about what Jane Austen's fatal illness really was, and no doubt there always will be.

Lydia glared at her sister once again. "The qualities you mention are womanly qualities. No man would admit to your list, especially on the Internet. Besides, as I told you before, a stupid man is probably better than an ugly man. To choose, look at the pictures, and later, when you are with one of them, you must use your imagination to make him a whole being. I have never met a living man comprised of all your qualities. No one man would appear in every category if you could search so."

The next day, the sisters checked Elizabeth's Matchmaker account. A Mr. Wickham, who looked handsome enough, invited her to dinner. He added, "Although I am often shy and awkward in crowds, those who know me the best, my servants and my sister, will attest that I am a kind, good man. My silence in public has been mistaken for pride, yet I hope for a fortunate chance to show my true self to you."

A Mr. Darcy wrote, "Nothing pleases me more than a good amount of company. Please come with me to the upcoming ball."

Lydia proclaimed, "Oh, Mr. Darcy's countenance is pleasing."

Elizabeth rushed a reply before she lost her nerve. She accepted both invitations. To Mr. Darcy she wrote, "I should like to dance with a man handsome as you. Such a partner will keep me from feeling jealous of other women the entire evening."

To Mr. Wickham she wrote, "In private, I should enjoy a man with depth of soul, for marital ongoings remain concealed by discreet people."

Lydia was not unamused.

"We shall see," Elizabeth answered, "which one is prideful, and against him I shall be prejudiced."

⌒ Samosas and Sensibility ⌒
SAYANTANI DASHGUPTA

The family of DashGupta had been long settled in Parsippany, New Jersey. Well, since Mr. DashGupta got sponsored for his green card back in 1988 and managed to convince the INS to grant Mrs. DashGupta a spousal visa, that is.

Their residence had initially been in the Indian enclave of the Sussex Gardens Apartment Complex off Route 46, but as Mrs. DashGupta was from a distinguished and old, if ridiculously impoverished, Bengali family, the rough society, marked by the sounds of Punjabi bhangra booming through souped-up car stereos, was quite more than her poor nerves could bear. Having a healthy respect for his wife's nerves, Mr. DashGupta transferred his wife and infant daughters posthaste—or rather, as soon as he was financially able, to the decidedly middle class subdivision of Norland Estates. There, for almost two decades, the DashGuptas had lived in an unremarkable medium-sized McMansion, in so respectable a manner as to be completely unknown by their surrounding acquaintances.

On weekends, in the dank basements of South Jersey community centers, the DashGupta daughters acquired all the requisite accomplishments of young Bengali ladies. They gained a thorough knowledge of Rabindra Sangeet music, singing, and dancing; they learned to read, write, and naturally speak their mother tongue; but besides all this, they gained something in their air, their manner of walking, their tone of voice, and expressions so as to suggest an impeccably South Asian, if slightly anachronistic, capacity, application, and elegance. And while these traits may have left lesser young women adrift in the rigid society of American high school, the DashGupta girls had such a pleasantness of manner and address, such a generosity of spirit, as to endear them to at least a close circle of their classmates.

Which is not to say the sisters resembled one another entirely. Ellora, the elder daughter, possessed a strength of understanding and quickness of intellect that placed her consistently on the Parsippany High School honor roll, in addition to granting her the pleasant success of several state championships in debate, elocution, and mathematics. And while such qualities might have relegated most young ladies to guaranteed spinsterhood, Ellora possessed as well a pair of fine, dark eyes in a remarkably pretty face. Though only seventeen, her teachers predicted early admission to any of several distinguished universities. Her mother, meanwhile, rested her hopes on an early marriage to a man of rank and fortune, which, for Mrs. DashGupta, meant a doctor or an engineer, naturally.

Mallika's abilities were, in many respects, quite equal to her sister's. She was sensible and clever, although her extracurricular activities tended toward the dramatic and performing arts. At sixteen, she had an excessive fondness for vixenish nail polish, glittery body powder, and temporary henna tattoos. Although her face and form held less classical grace than Ellora's, she made up for this potential deficit with extravagant joie de vivre and a violence of emotion. She either loved or despaired, delighted or wept. In other words, she was quite at the mercy of her hormones, much to the affliction of the less-likely-to-get-pregnant Ellora.

And so the sisters might have finished their high school careers—one full of sense, the other, sensibility—if fate had not intervened in the form of a massive myocardial infarction that resulted in the ill-timed death of their beloved father, Mr. DashGupta, whilst at his software company desk. To compound the family's bereavement, it was soon discovered that, consistent with extended family traditions, the house and all their worldly assets had been left, not to Mrs. DashGupta or her daughters, but rather, to her porcine-proportioned brother-in-law, one Mr. Mohondash DashGupta—to whom his younger brother had naively entrusted the care of his beloved wife and offspring.

But the elder Mr. DashGupta was a man of mean understanding and meaner temperament, whose fortune had been made in the unseemly business of (gasp) trade. Indeed, although Mrs. DashGupta was loath to mention it in her decidedly white-collar social circles, her brother-in-law in fact owned the largest chain of Indian beauty salons in the tristate area.

No sooner were the funerary rituals over than did Mr. Mohondash DashGupta arrive at Norland Estates, with his dyspeptic wife, delinquent children, and cantankerous mother-in-law in tow. So acutely did Mrs. DashGupta feel this ungracious behavior, and so did she despise the mother-in-law for making her cook all the time, that she determined to quit the house immediately.

"It was my brother's last request to me," said Mr. Mohondash DashGupta with something like a leer in his eye, "to assist his widow and daughters."

"He did not know what he was talking about, that lightheaded loafer!" exclaimed the mother-in-law with a gaseous belch. "What better assistance than jobs for these three good-for-nothings in one of your beauty salons?"

And so it was that Ellora, Mallika, and their distraught mother became employed as beauticians at Eyebrows-R-Us, the latest of their uncle's empire of beauty salons, specializing in eyebrow (and, for the exceedingly hirsute, upper-lip, chin, and whole face) threading.

Beauty was indeed in the eye(brow) of the beholder.

DID YOU KNOW?

There are around 160 letters written by Jane Austen that are still in existence today, and most contain everyday family news, much of it about small domestic matters—new furniture, dress material, plants in the garden, weather. The health and welfare of various family members is related and discussed seriously or comically as the situation dictates. This being Jane Austen, the playful remarks are imaginative and witty. There is gossip about neighbors, some of it quite sharp. Some rude, even vulgar, jokes have survived. Austen sometimes reveals exasperation and depression, sometimes optimism and joy. The letters contain frequent expressions of deep affection for family and friends that are eloquent and moving.

As R.W. Chapman, the great editor of Jane Austen's writings, points out, Jane's letters to Cassandra are more focused on the "business of news," whereas other correspondents more fully inspire the "flow of fancy." Indeed, the letters to her nieces and her nephew James-Edward are delightfully imaginative and amusing. Even the trivial everyday matters found in the letters are fascinating reading for anyone with an interest in Jane Austen.

Destitute in Dubai
RABAB HAMZA

It is a truth universally acknowledged that a Dubai building, in possession of a superlative height, must be the most sought-after address in town.

However little known the merits or conveniences of such a building may be on its first entering the market, this truth is so well fixed in the minds of the jet set, that no sooner were plans for the world's tallest building, the Burj Khalifa, announced than it was considered as the rightful property of one or other of Dubai's elite.

It was the year 2006, and among the more glittering of Dubai's haut monde was a young couple by the name of Elton. Brad and Angie Elton, clever, handsome, and rich, in possession of lucrative jobs and indulgent bosses, and always on the lookout for ways to best showcase their wealth and standing, were just the kind of people to be impressed by the marketing campaign for the world's highest man-made structure.

"My dear soul mate," said his lord to Angie one day, "have you heard that Burj Khalifa apartments are to be sold at last? Though the building is not to be completed until 2009, they have put up the residential units for sale."

Mrs. Elton replied that she had not heard.

"But they have," returned he, "and the Burj is being described as a vertical city; an engineering marvel. What a fine thing for our reputation."

"How so? How can our reputation be affected?"

"My dear angel," replied her husband, "how can you be so tiresome? You must know that I am thinking of our buying one of them."

Mrs. Elton readily agreed, and happy for all their material feelings was the day they got rid of the best part of their fortune and became the proud off-the-plan owners of a one-bedroom apartment at the most prestigious address in Dubai, and consequently the whole of the UAE.

With what delighted pride they afterward visited their friends, and talked of the design plans for their newest acquisition, may be guessed. "It is just what an apartment ought to be," said Mrs. Elton, "grand, spacious, luxurious, and I never saw such happy surroundings! So many swimming pools and amenities, with such perfect architecture!"

"It also seems handsome," said her friend, Elizabeth, "which an apartment ought likewise to be, if it possibly can. Its excellence is thereby complete. I give you leave to like it. You have liked many a stupider investment."

Armed with the lavish praise of most of their friends and acquaintances, and not at all deterred by the apparently envious calls to prudence and caution by the rest, the Eltons, possessed of a dual income and no encumbrances, decided that their happiness only needed the purchase of an adjoining apartment in the same building to be complete.

Not possessed of the wherewithal to effect such a purchase on their own, the two had no option but to approach the banks, which were only too happy at that time, in the year six, to finance all the extravagant whims and profligate fancies of the real estate speculators.

Heavily burdened by debt, and struggling to make their mortgage payments on time, the young couple was yet hopeful of the future and looked forward to a time when their investments would appreciate in value and fulfill all their aspirations.

Alas, it was not to be. The economic recession of the year eight, the crumbling real estate market, and the global financial crisis were all equally against them. The value of the apartments plunged by half, they lost their jobs, the banks threatened to foreclose, their maxed-out credit cards offered no solace, and the two had no choice but to abandon their bank-financed BMWs at the airport and flee to the faraway shores of their home countries.

Time passed, and though inadvertently delayed, the opening of Burj Khalifa was held in the year ten. As the Eltons watched the glittering opening ceremony on their television screen, which featured an extravagant display of fireworks, sound, and light and water effects, they breathed a sigh of regret and wished that they had heeded their friends' advice and limited their ambition within the bounds of what was practicable and feasible.

However dismal might be the end to the promised brilliancy of their career, the developers of the property yet succeeded in what they had set out to do. I therefore leave it to be settled, by whomsoever it may concern, whether the tendency of this work be altogether to recommend fiscal prudence in individuals or reward extravagant ambition in developers.

⌒ Pursuit ⌒
PATRICIA RICHARDS

It is a fact very rarely vocalized that a wealthy, divorced gentleman will be pursued—in a dignified manner—by any recently divorced female greatly in search of a more salubrious experience of matrimony, and that this gentleman will also be pursued by any single female with an eye keenly on the lookout for a prospect who might lead to potentially comfortable circumstances.

Such is the situation of Mr. Howard, whose circumstance, whispered to be considerable, has attracted the quite speculative attentions of one Miss Harrington-Davis, who, certain of her attractions and quite determined, has decided that she must be the next Mrs. Howard. Miss Harrington-Davis, it might be noted, is quietly rumored to have moved from the far reaches of the county to be within close hailing distance of Mr. Howard's not-inconsiderable residence, and such industriousness begged quiet, prompt attention from those members of a society concerned with such interesting happenings.

Alas, Mr. Howard appeared to be somewhat partial to one Miss Alexander, who, unorthodox and unconventional, has unexpectedly captured his attention and perplexed his soul, much to Miss Harrington-Davis's displeasure and Miss Alexander's quiet bemusement. For, while Mr. Howard would be an unexpected and not unpleasant addition to Miss Alexander's life, his conventional and orthodox lifestyle would somewhat hamper Miss Alexander's preference for an unconventional and unorthodox experience of the world.

Such is the complex setting to a summer evening's unvoiced deliberations, masquerading beneath the pretext of an informal midsummer's repast.

While Miss Harrington-Davis holds court with her supporters, gaily running her fingers through her well-teased hair, her tinkling laughter floats softly around the gathering as she ensures that its melody will reach and assuredly enchant Mr. Howard's musically inclined ears. Miss Alexander, well loved in her own society, is surrounded by confidants who quietly support her supposed candidacy. Unmoved by the silent tempest of wills surrounding her, Miss Alexander, with some restraint, quietly inhales the delicate, fruity notes of an exceptional Indian tea and listens as an acquaintance regales her with tales replete with the antics of a precocious grandchild.

Mr. Howard, meanwhile, somewhat overwhelmed by his confusion, welcomes and sees to the comfort of his guests, ensuring that all are enraptured by the magnanimity of his generous hospitality, and tries to avoid stealing glances at the delightfully unconventional Miss Alexander, as Miss Harrington-Davis's tinkling laughter becomes a bit louder and her unnaturally gray eyes sparkle with dubious joy.

Maximilian, a chocolate Labrador much beloved by Mr. Howard and self-proclaimed master of this home, lazily enters the gathering, sauntering over to bid Mr. Howard a quiet, canine "Good Evening," who himself makes much ado over his furry, four-legged friend. Miss Harrington-Davis, suddenly aware of an unequaled opportunity to endear herself to her host, squeals in a throaty, ladylike manner and rushes across to gush untold enthusiasm over the four-legged wonder. Maximilian, a little surprised at the squealing human, gently disengages himself from her frothy sounds and backs away to peer curiously at her from behind the safety of his owner's expensively trousered legs.

Miss Alexander, attention caught by the persistent yet escalating squeals, watches as Maximilian seeks the further safety of the fireplace, pausing on his journey to wag his tail gently at the genuine smile she bestows upon him. He, enchanted by this orderly display of affection, gently woofs and takes a detour to venture over for a tickle from this purveyor of quiet dignity.

⤳ Caroline's Humiliation Conga ⤳
CELTICGIRL13

William's Journal

Today was very interesting to say the least. Charles, Jane, Elizabeth, and I all went to the Museum of Fine Arts. Will and I were about to go into another exhibit when my phone vibrated.

"Caroline?" I asked.

Caroline said, "Is it true? Are Charles and Jane engaged?"

I shrugged my shoulders. "I guess. He was planning on proposing today, but that's supposed to be a secret. If you want to give them your congratulations, they're in the Museum of Fine Arts. Probably in the Impressionist section."

About ten minutes later, Elizabeth and I were checking out the Egyptian art exhibition when Caroline walked in to find us, with my arms around Elizabeth's waist.

"Caroline . . ." I said. "We were just admiring the latest in international art."

"I thought you were here to see Charles and Jane," Elizabeth said.

"I already saw them," Caroline said. "It's quite shocking, however, to see you here, Elizabeth."

"Why should it be shocking?" Elizabeth said. "I'm his girlfriend!"

"You're kidding, right?" Caroline said. She looked like she was going to burst into a pillar of flames at any second.

"Uh, he has his arms around my waist," Elizabeth said. "Can it be any clearer that we're going out?"

I chuckled.

"But I thought . . ." We knew Caroline couldn't lose her temper in front of everybody in the museum, so I told Elizabeth to let me talk to Caroline privately. I led her to another part of the museum. Caroline began her ramble as soon as Elizabeth was out of earshot. "William, surely you two are playing some prank on me like you did in March. You are the springtime I dreamed of so desperate during the cold winter chills. Contempt, farewell! And maiden pride, adieu! No glory lives behind the back of such. I will requite thee, William, and my feelings will not be repressed. I love you. Most ardently."

It was all I could do not to laugh. Not only did she take a quote from my favorite play completely out of context, but it seems like her knowledge of *Pride and Prejudice* extended only to the Keira Knightley movie.

I replied, "You are too hasty, Miss. You forget that I have made no answer. Let me do it without further loss of time. Accept my thanks for the compliments you are paying me. I am very sensible of the honor of your proposal, but I have no choice but to decline it." I looked to Elizabeth who was recording all this on her video phone.

"William, I don't understand. I'm so much better than this chit is. I graduated from one of the top-ranked high schools in

California with honors. I've already graduated from UCLA cum laude with a degree in liberal arts. I'm in grad school to get my MBA, and if nothing else, I have better cars than her. She, on the other hand, cusses too much, has no job offers or even a real job, a dysfunctional family, no style, and a pickup truck, which she shares with her sister. Besides all that, think about what everyone in your social circle would say if you married a redneck."

I rolled my eyes. "You've said enough, Caroline. You've insulted Elizabeth and me in every possible manner. Elizabeth is my girl-friend. I never liked you in the way you wanted me to because you're too much of a kiss-up and a wannabe. Now please go home and never bug me about Elizabeth again or I'll tell certain CEOs about your rudeness."

I almost felt sorry for her until she screamed that I'd be crawl-ing back for her and that Elizabeth would be sorry. Elizabeth posted the video on YouTube the next day to the delight of our fellow coworkers. Needless to say, Caroline won't be invited to Charles and Jane's wedding.

⌒ Willoughby's Boogie Nights ⌒
STACEY GRAHAM

Light bounced off the disco ball like tiny diamonds shattering on the gold lamé dress pants hugging the aerobics-toned legs of Willoughby. Long-limbed and nimble as a tiger, he prowled the dance floor at the Holiday Inn Scandals in search of a partner, his platform boots clicked on the parquet floor in rhythm to the beat of Donna Summer's soulful siren call about the last dance for the desperate and slightly sweaty. Spying the cascading curls of a young woman across the room, he gyrated her way, his intent clear—their hands must touch, their breath to mingle; they must speak each other's unspoken language.

DID YOU KNOW?

If a person has heard anything at all about Jane Austen's mother, it is probably that she was a hypochondriac. That seems to be true, but there is much more to be told about Mrs. Austen, the intriguing woman with whom Jane lived her entire life.

For all her aristocratic and scholarly background, Mrs. Austen's practical streak and lack of concern with appearances served her well as the wife of a country clergyman and farmer with a very modest income. She jokes in a letter to her sister-in-law, after saying how she would like to show off her children, that she would like to show off her other "riches," too—her bull, cows, ducks, and chickens.

She was not only a mother to eight children of her own, but she also seems to have done quite well mothering her husband's pupils firmly but fairly, looking after their meals and laundry and their characters, too. Mrs. Austen wrote poetry from childhood on, and we have some of her very clever light verse, including the poems she regularly wrote to these boys. The verses are charming and spirited—and often relayed a specific message—and evidently meant enough to her charges that they preserved them their whole lives so that we can enjoy them today.

Like so many women in Jane Austen's novels, Mrs. Austen was a strong, confident woman. She could be stubborn, and she sometimes made tart remarks about the neighbors—as did Jane (in private, of course). Even after she fell seriously ill in Bath, she recovered to write a cheerful, defiant poem called "Dialogue between Death & Mrs. Austen."

After she was widowed, Mrs. Austen took pleasure in visiting her relatives, taking along her daughters. At Stoneleigh Abbey she counted the windows (forty-five) and described the grand rooms with enthusiasm and a novelist's imagination and eye for detail.

Marianne's eyes slid toward him, her tongue chasing the plastic straw around the rim of her Shirley Temple. Cocking her head, she motioned to her sister, Elinor, that they were soon to have a visitor.

"Here comes another one. At least this one can dance. The last one trod on my foot and broke a strap." Extending her floppy stiletto-clad toes toward Elinor as evidence, Marianne sighed in resignation to her fate of turning down another would-be Lothario.

"Madam, I would be honored if you would extend me the pleasure of the next dance. I believe I hear the strains of 'Boogie Wonderland' from the DJ booth." His dark eyes caressed her face like wandering fingers of love; his hand trembled with anticipation as he reached for the fair beauty.

"Good sir, I'm afraid I cannot boogie at the moment. My strap is such that it is quite impossible for me to get funky on the dance floor," said Marianne, waving her foot.

"Fear not, I shall transport you to the pinnacle of 'Funky Town' and return you unharmed before 'Stayin' Alive.'"

Before she could protest, Willoughby carried Marianne to the dance floor. Together they flailed about to "YMCA," piggybacked "The Hustle," and couldn't stop till they got enough.

"Enough, kind sir! I am quite fatigued by your exertions. Leave me be by my sullen older sister who has had nary a dance," said Marianne. Adjusting her mesh tube top, Marianne then pointed back to her table where Elinor glared in the darkness. Willoughby acquiesced; he knew she'd return for more of the Will-man.

"As you wish, Madam." Crossing the dance floor with such beauty in his arms, Willoughby rested his cheek upon her head briefly, breathing in the scent of Charlie mixed with Jean Naté After Bath Splash. It was a heady combination.

"Sir, your tenderness has moved me, not to mention your impressive splits on the dance floor. Mayhap you will call on me next week? We can watch *Friday Night Videos* and read poetry." Her voice loud over the speaker system, Marianne dared to hope he wouldn't notice the tremor that shook her though she trembled in his arms.

"Miss Marianne, I would be delighted . . . but I've been called away by my aunt for the season. I don't know when I'll return again to Scandals, though it now holds my heart." Pain edged his voice, his passion to boogie now checked by the whims of an old woman.

"Then we must return once more to the dance floor so that we can remember each other in depressing sonnets until you once more return to me."

Throwing her arms wide, she narrowly missed another couple getting down on the edge of the dance floor. "Oh, those Wickhams! Always drawing attention to themselves because that's the way (uh huh, uh huh) they like it."

Dropping Marianne's tan pantyhosed feet to the floor, Willoughby drew her in close, being careful not to entangle her curls with the enormous amount of chest hair escaping his unbuttoned shirt. As Lydia Wickham did the Worm on the lighted floor behind them, Willoughby and Marianne held each other, saying their final goodbyes to the beat of "Super Freak" before separating into the night.

"Call me, okay?" Marianne yelled across the parking lot. Elinor rolled her eyes and searched for the key to the Ford Pinto.

"Yeah . . . sure." A hand gestured in her direction as Willoughby unlocked the El Camino's door. "Till we meet again, fair Carrie Ann!" With a roar of the V6 engine, Willoughby sped into the night.

"That's Marianne, you jerk," she whispered.

"Come on, let's get a Slurpee," Elinor offered.

"I believe you're looking for this, Madam." The voice behind her made Elinor pause. Turning, she saw an outstretched palm with her car key nestled in the manly folds.

"Thank you," she stumbled.

"Edward. And I enjoy Slurpees as well. May I accompany you?" Folding Elinor's hand within the crook of his arm, Edward said, "I see a 7-11 a few blocks down. Shall we walk?" As Elinor smiled through Marianne's pout, she escorted Edward to the convenience store and into his heart.

Black Ops Bennets
RILEY REDGATE

In the pursuit of a greater sensibility and a distinct taste of modernism to which few of his wealthier acquaintances had not yet adhered, Mr. Darcy found himself in possession of a marvelous entertainment, which was soon pronounced quite agreeable by Mr. Bingley.

"I am most partial to the clarity of the image this game produces," cried Bingley. "However, I find myself confounded as to which weapon I hold. The appearances of these weapons bear little distinction! It is a callous error on behalf of the programmers, is it not?"

"Whichever weapon has been bestowed upon your character, it must be esteemed useful, as it provides to you a Kill Count of magnificent stature, which, until this happy find, had been but a wistful dream," Darcy remarked dryly.

A prepared surety appeared to descend upon Darcy then, as a creature undeniably undead made its progression across the screen, which faced the two men. Said Darcy, "Shall I press the key marked B, or that upon which is inscribed the letter A?" In his inquiry was a frantic appeal, for the undead creature had held up its hands and begun its dragging approach toward the camera.

"Both," said Bingley, and, as gunfire erupted, excitement extended itself across his visage. Never before Black Ops had any invention borne such joy to mankind! How should any day be spent away from this uncommon satisfaction?

Scarcely had the excitement bestowed itself on Bingley, however, before it receded in light of a most unhappy realization; his attention had fixated upon a script hovering above the heads of two players whose curious monikers read "E_pWnz" and "J_mOnEy." Bingley felt drawn to comment on the script, in turn compelling Darcy to seek the source of such a dismayed tone as that issuing from his friend.

Remarked Bingley, "A pair of players in the realms of virtual skirmish have called us 'n00bs,' and I am thus inclined to forestall assistance when next the undead barrage them."

"I am inclined to respond in a similar manner," said Darcy. "I often find that petty revenges like to that which you suggest are the pleasantest options when faced with such impudence."

They continued, though the impudent players absented themselves before further attacks. After the passing of some time, both men were surprised by the sudden appearance in the room of

Elizabeth and Jane, the virulent rage of whom seemed beyond adequate expression.

Elizabeth knew not how she might chastise the despicable behaviour of the two gentlemen; they had scarcely emerged from this chamber for innumerable hours! "Mr. Darcy," cried she, "I must protest against this condemnable obsession to which you seem practically married! If it be not too much of a distraction, I might remind you of to whom your vows were spoken!"

But Darcy and Bingley found themselves distracted instead by a renewed wave of undead warriors, and the unhappy sisters found themselves bathed in a most uncouth silence hardly befitting of two married couples. Jane cast a longing glance to Bingley, but her husband was too overcome by the amiable nature of Black Ops to realize what scrutiny he bore.

When Elizabeth next spoke, it was with cold repugnance. "I had hoped that our taunt would offend your pride in a sufficient quantity to cause you to disavow this game and all it entails, but I see I was mistaken."

Darcy spared a trifling glance to Elizabeth. "To what taunt do you refer, Elizabeth?"

Now a wicked glint appeared in Elizabeth's eye; her countenance bore a strange mischief whose presence was quite unfamiliar to Darcy. "I, too, respond to the Call of Duty," said Elizabeth. "I find myself thoroughly unchallenged by its petty trials. When, however, I do endeavour to entertain myself in such a base manner, I may pick up the controller in the drawing room and sign myself in as my chosen name: 'E_pWnz.'"

Jane made a simple attempt at disguising laughter as a cough; the subsequent expressions of the two men were utterly woebegone and quite pitiful to behold.

"N00bs you deemed us!" cried Bingley. "Jane—were you to do with this foolhardiness? This cruelty?"

"This is outrage," declared Darcy simply, a fearful darkness descending on his disposition.

Jane fervently denied any involvement, meriting such a scornful glance from Elizabeth that she relented almost instantly. "I admit—I am J_mOnEy. Oh! Lizzy and I meant no poor conduct! I hope you do not find us to be the sole instigators of outrage, Mr. Darcy."

Darcy shook his head with an unhappy solemnity. "It is not your deceit that I find detestable."

A grave silence hung over the room.

Finished Darcy, "It is rather the fact that either of your Kill Counts may be observed to be higher than mine and Mr. Bingley's—combined!"

⟶ Status and Social Networking ⟵
Mary C.M. Phillips

Elizabeth, having had prior feelings of reservation, could not help fancying the thought of opening a Facebook account and related her curiosity to Jane.

"Indeed," said Jane, smiling. "The gentlemen on Facebook you will find to be agreeable and pleasant; men of fine reputation and good manners."

Elizabeth's disinclination was noticeable; she was silent. She considered her feelings of possible judgment. "What might Mr. Darcy think of such an act?"

"Mr. Darcy is not so well worth your consideration, for he is most disagreeable," Mrs. Bennet protested from across the breakfast-parlour. "So proud and conceited; I detest the man. How pleasant it is to spend time with Mr. Collins, instead, a lively gentlemen of the finest breeding with ties to Wall Street, and having made a bucket-load of money hedging crude oil and gold bullion; he is clever and well-suited!"

Elizabeth left the breakfast-parlour where all but Jane and Mr. Bennet were assembled, gathered her thoughts, and sat down in the library where Mr. Bennet spent late afternoons playing games of leisure on his laptop, such as Mafia Wars and Farmville.

He, too, had been headstrong and less than enthusiastic to involve himself with proud activities such as social networking until Mrs. Bennet explained that her nerves could simply bear no more.

She related to him that the neighbors were frequently tagging photos of Mr. Bennet, a handsome but rather large man, onto her Wall, photos of him playing electric guitar with his band, Good and Amiable Company.

"My dear, you must indeed get your own account and have compassion on my nerves," she cried. He had always intended to open an account, so while his wife visited the Bingley home one fine afternoon, he signed up thither.

Elizabeth logged on to Mr. Bennet's computer and pondered this new adventure with much attention. Opening a Facebook account could be pleasant and satisfying! She reflected on the prospect of reuniting with friends from high school and abroad, as the Internet was vast and enormous, a place containing a great variety of ground, a place to perhaps even write a blog—or sell crap on eBay. Oh, the possibilities!

With a few keystrokes she had registered herself and entered the world of social networking, looking upon ladies of fashionable attire, well-groomed and handsome gentlemen, less-than-well-groomed and handsome gentlemen, and some less-than-handsome and in need of a bath.

Suddenly a red spot appeared on the top of the screen. Elizabeth promptly clicked the unannounced e-mail. Here she found a "friendship request" from Mr. Darcy himself. "Will you accept my friendship, as my feelings have not changed since I saw you last?"

Elizabeth was elated. The decision had been a good and proper one. She confirmed his request, as any lady of good character and happy manners would, and then spent the rest of the evening viewing photos that he had recently posted of Pemberley Woods.

He had not a profile photo, however, as both Elizabeth and he agreed was far too pompous, lacking humility.

Elizabeth had also entered "it's complicated" in reference to her relationship status. Soon, however, within a fortnight, she would be updating her status to "in-a-relationship" with none other than the handsome, although privately so, Mr. Darcy.

Did You Know?

With five brothers at home and just one sister, Jane was growing up in quite a masculine household. Moreover, her parents ran a school for boys in their home. Is it any wonder Jane Austen was able to depict the behavior of men with such accuracy and their feelings with such sympathy?

We see how much the dispositions and preferred pastimes of spirited boys must have appealed to the young Jane in the characters of some of her heroines. Catherine Morland, the heroine of *Northanger Abbey*, is in fact what we would call a tomboy: "She was fond of all boys' plays, and greatly preferred cricket not merely to dolls, but to the more heroic enjoyments of infancy . . . she was moreover noisy and wild, hated confinement and cleanliness, and loved nothing so well in the world as rolling down the green slope at the back of the house." As many have pointed out, there is just such a slope at the back of the Steventon rectory.

Bennet Bridezillas
TARA O'DONNELL

It has become a truth universally acknowledged that a successful television network, possessed of the need to keep their rating status on a high level, must be in want of an entertainment dedicated to strife.

Bearing that notion in mind, the Royal We Channel is pleased to extend an invitation to its gentle viewers to accompany them as they pay a call upon the Bennets of Longbourn during their preparations for the upcoming nuptials of one of their five daughters.

Do join us in celebration as well as speculation into the goings-on amongst this seemingly happy family as they gather together to create a splendid occasion that should bring their best behavior forth or, for the benefit of our mutual amusement, reveal some of their less attractive qualities:

(As the curtain rises, Mrs. Bennet and Mr. Collins are seated near one another in the parlor while Mr. Bennet keeps to his book nearby.)

Mrs. Bennet: Oh, my dear Mr. Bennet, is it not wonderful that just as our dear Lydia was finished mourning the loss of poor Mr. Wickham than she should find herself engaged to that charming Colonel Fitzwilliam, who has quite a good income for a second son, and a relation of our dear Mr. Darcy as well?

Mr. Bennet: Quite true, my dear. Our youngest is indeed most fortunate to have found another man with a taste for silly women and enough of a fortune to make such a union worth her while. (He turns away from visitors, book firmly in front of his face.)

Mrs. B: Oh, how you take delight in vexing me and my poor nerves! (She turns her attention to Mr. Collins.) And how fortunate for our family that one of your parish duties is now as arranger of weddings, Mr. Collins!

Mr. Collins: Yes, madam, the banns for your daughter's marriage could not have been called at a more suitable time. With the assistance of my dear Charlotte, along with my noble patroness Lady Catherine de Bourgh, whose sanction I would not dare to proceed without. . . .

(Mr. Collins's lofty statements regarding his new employ are interrupted by the fierce opening of the parlor door and the entrance of Lydia with her sister, Kitty, alongside her. Mr. Bennet chooses to take this most agreeable opportunity to make haste to his library.)

Kitty: The gowns that Lydia has chosen for her wedding party to wear are a hideous colour that makes me look ill, Mamma! Have her change it, I beg of you!

Lydia: It is not my fault that you are too plain to look well enough in it! There is not a prettier shade in satin in all of Brighton, and when my dear Fitzwilliam wears his regimentals amongst all the officers attending our wedding there, that colour must match his blue coat!

Mrs. B: Have some compassion on my poor nerves!

Mr. Collins: I was not informed that Brighton would be the location for your wedding, cousin. Lady Catherine was condescending enough to allow Rosings to be used for the reception, provided that certain restrictions are adhered to.

Mrs. B: Why, that is very good of her Ladyship to make her house available, Sir, but Rosings is quite a long ways away. Now, I was considering Purvis Lodge, despite their dreadful attics or . . .

(The former Mrs. Wickham chooses this moment to make her displeasure at such arrangements known by raising the tone of her voice to such heights as to cause the furniture to tremble while stamping her feet.)

Lydia: I WANT TO GO TO BRIGHTON!!!

(Kitty begins to weep and flees from the limited comfort her mother can provide at this particular time. As she ascends the stairs, her elder sister Elizabeth can be seen speaking with their father outside of the library door.)

Elizabeth: Father, I entreat you, it is bad enough that Lydia's impudent behavior is known outside her family, but to have this most public exposure while she is in the midst of preparing to make a new beginning for herself and Colonel Fitzwilliam will only serve to fix her in society as the most determinedly foolish bride that ever chose to reenter the married state!

Mr. B: Calm yourself, my dear. It is true that Lydia seems to have learned little about proper decorum during her earlier marriage, but do remember what I told you once about being sport for our neighbors and laughing at them in return, which sadly seems to be the fashion these days. . . .

(Our presence has been detected by Elizabeth and her father, causing them both to retreat into the quiet sanctuary of the library and firmly close the door behind them. Perhaps they will excuse our interference at a later time and realize that it was kindly meant.)

Sass and Sexual Ambiguity
STACEY SPENCER

Elizabeth and Emma were neither above the age of graduation nor below the age of menstruation, and were in possession of a notable tendency to enjoy the taste of Pimm's and not stray away from even the most altering of mind-numbing pharmaceuticals. To their well-below-favorably-rated credit, they had recently gained acquisition of a fine Ford Taurus, which aided them in setting out to drive to the end of the world or, as their fellow countrymen called it, California.

One would not say that it wasn't true that they had set out to visit a vacationing friend, a man who had gone to college and left, then returned to college only to be released again and come back with a condition called PhD. At university, Elizabeth had been acquainted with this PhD while not dabbling in Sapphic Arts and Literature, and it wouldn't be untrue to say that she had also, in an unwittingly ambitious way, attracted a condition of her own, also named with its own three-letter acronym, from him.

Ooh! He angered her so with his crotchetiness that her chest would heave at the very thought of him. He, with his bad taste and conservative ways, was no match for a wild and untamed thing such as herself. One would be unwise or unobservant to say that her motivations for this visit, though murky with the unhinged emotion of a single woman who was inebriated and had not been to bed in several weeks, might have included a plan lesser than to kill him with kindness.

But, oh my, how her bitter tune changed once she caught sight of his palatial pleasure dome! The velvet fainting couch! Rotating bed with optional harness and chains! Purple and leopard-print window dressings—the height of her own tastes and such magnificent display of the man she did not know he was! And his bookshelves! They were filled to the brim with stories that had captured her youthful heart: *The Kama Sutra*, *The Story of O*, and—gasp!—*The Happy Hooker*.

His place was the perfect blend of sass and sexual ambiguity she had been secretly waiting for her entire life! She hadn't considered marriage before (particularly not to a man after finding Emma), but after a night with his frisky servants and Olympian-like playmate, how could she not consider?

When he finally arrived at the party, he serenaded her with a lovely song about from whence he came. She had never been serenaded before and felt a ping of jealousy from Emma. But she would do well to find her own man now and live the kind of life that Elizabeth now cherished, with white picket fences adorned with velvet drapery and electric barbed wire.

There was such a fuss between the two girls on the car ride home concerning Elizabeth's newfound fondness for Dr. Darcy.

"Surely, you don't take the professor seriously. I mean, think of your family."

"I wouldn't think they'd mind much, since he has a large house and servants. What do you have?"

"I think he must have put some kind of spell on you. It's as if you're dreaming."

"Oh, I shouldn't not say but that I felt as if I might be. Could it be the effect of some kind of magical spell or power that Dr. Darcy has me under? Could it be I have fallen in love?"

"Most likely it's the poor mock imitation of Pimm's we consumed during the revelry last night. Given the host's affinity for madness, I'd not be surprised if he hadn't heightened our drunk with hallucinogens."

"I say it's not a crime, to dream and to want more. That's what I say, 'Thou shall not dream it, though must be it.'"

"Now you're being just plain childish and foolish. Really, get your feet on the ground and look at the rational evidence. What has he done to you?"

"I don't know, but I definitely feel different. Wait—what's this? Could it be?" She lifted the hem of her jacket and skirt to reveal a fishnet-stocking-clad leg. "I doth believe I feel quite sexy."

⌁ Virtue and Voracity ⌁
JENNIFER HARGIS

Eleven men stood on each side of one of the lines that had been drawn on the lawn. The gentlemen on one side were wearing red regimentals, while the others wore white. As they assembled in an orderly manner and bent over, those who wore white snarled at those who wore red and the men in red did likewise.

Mr. Jonathan Higney-Pickering looked straight ahead at Mr. Andrew Wilerman and said, "Good day, Mr. Wilerman. I have it on excellent authority that your mother is of questionable reputation."

At which point Mr. Wilerman became warm and stated that Mr. Higney-Pickering was of no consequence and his information was unsound.

Further down the line Mr. Henry Fitzgammon took the opportunity to express the following to Mr. Thomas Badhusband: "Good sir, I will shortly run toward you with great speed, thrust you to the ground, and trample upon your hindquarters." Mr. Badhusband took no offense, but rather smiled and invited Mr. Fitzgammon to try.

There was an oddly shaped ball on the ground, and one of the gentlemen in red reached down to touch it as the gentleman behind him, who was standing erect, began to shout with little concern for such ill behavior as would not befit a gentleman of his position. The man with his hand on the ball thrust it between his legs so that the gentleman behind him was forced to put his own hands out to catch it, lest he be injured.

This insufferable act set the gentlemen in white propelling themselves toward the men in red, as if all those in red were equally as responsible for holding the ball as the two gentlemen who had actually touched it. As promised, Mr. Fitzgammon did indeed thrust Mr. Badhusband to the ground and trample his hindquarters.

The gentleman in red, who had the ball, fearing for his safety, threw it to Mr. Higney-Pickering, who proceeded to run around, over, and under all of the men in white who stood before him and did not stop until he reached the area at the end of the lawn that had been colored red. Having ended his journey, he threw the accursed ball down and began to walk around it in much the manner that a chicken might.

Several men, who had been staying out of the way of the men in regimentals, began shouting and throwing yellow handker-chiefs on the lawn. It had become evident that Mr. Badhusband, now able to stand, had elected to retaliate against Mr. Fitzgam-mon, had grabbed the lower portion of Mr. Fitzgammon's head-dress, the part which he wore across his face, and pulled with such abrupt force as to cause injury to him. Because Mr. Badhusband was wearing white, the gentlemen in red determined that this incident was of less importance to them than the happy occasion that had been precipitated by Mr. Higney-Pickering's achieving the end of the lawn.

There was a great deal of excitement, which grew even more unseemly when Mr. Wilerman's mother ripped away the bodice of her gown and ran across the lawn, thus reinforcing Mr. Higney-Pickering's statement that she was indeed of questionable reputation.

DID YOU KNOW?

Many good writers are bad spellers, and Austen didn't have the benefit of computer programs to check her work for errors. But spelling was also not completely standardized in the eighteenth century, and people were more accepting of variations. Even proper names were sometimes spelled—or "spelt"—in different ways. In a famous reference to *Pride and Prejudice*, Austen wrote that she had "lop't and crop't" it—where we would insist on "lopped and cropped."

It might be distracting to read whole novels in which common nouns were capitalized in the old-fashioned style Austen frequently used, but some modern editions of Austen's texts bring every instance of her erratic and charming spelling into line with current usage, and so we also lose "Swisserland" and "ancle." Somehow Sophia's dying warning to Laura in *Love and Friendship*, "Run mad as often as you chuse; but do not faint," loses something when the spelling of the word "chuse" is updated. (Fanny Price, too, is amazed to find herself "a chuser of books.") The flavor of a different era is subtly retained with such details, whereas many writers of sequels to Austen's novels today, in the mistaken belief that such words are authentically "period" terms, use language that was archaic even in her time!

Because she wrote before the age of certain strict—and rather pedantic—grammatical rules, Jane Austen also makes what many today would deem grammatical errors, using "which" for "that" and "they" as a singular pronoun. (Many today are careful to say "he or she" rather than fall into that agreement "error.") However, we should also note that Austen cared enough about correct language to make use of it in her novels as a way of signaling character.

In *Northanger Abbey*, Henry Tilney jokes about ladies who have a "a very frequent ignorance of grammar," and his sister complains that he is always finding fault with her "for some incorrectness of language." He wittily complains about how the word "nice" has completely lost its original precise meaning and "now every commendation on every subject is comprised in that one word." (We might note that his complaint has lost none of its relevance.) Although he is being playful rather than serious and pedantic when he makes these remarks, he clearly does care about the way language is used. Henry Tilney is very closely identified with the author's attitude and opinions throughout the novel, so we can infer that Austen entered into his feelings on this subject, too.

One of the things that impresses Emma (to her surprise) about Harriet's would-be lover Robert Martin is the quality of the writing in the letter containing his marriage proposal: "There were not merely no grammatical errors, but as a composition it would not have disgraced a gentleman." Of course, Emma must talk herself out of this approbation in order to keep her predetermined opinion of him as "illiterate and vulgar." Lucy Steele in *Sense and Sensibility* truly is vulgar, and her speech is littered with grammatical errors: "It would have gave me such pleasure," "It would have been such a great pity to have went away," and "Anne and me are to go."

Lydia Bennet has grown up in the same household as articulate, eloquent Elizabeth and Jane, whose speech is grammatically correct, but she is quite different from her sisters in a number of ways. It is no coincidence that Lydia, who risks ruining herself and disgracing her entire family by living with a man outside of marriage, also says things like, "Mrs. Forster and me are such friends."

Incorrect, imprecise, vulgar language is a clear reflection of character in Jane Austen's writing, but the same cannot necessarily be said regarding speech that is entirely but merely correct, which might indicate nothing more than a good education.

Pride and Paparazzi
WENDY SIMARD

When Paris and Nicky were alone, the former, who had been cautious in her praise of Justin Bieber before, expressed to her sister how very much she admired him.

"He is just what a young man ought to be," said she, "sensible, good humoured, lively; and I never saw such happy manners!—so much ease, with such perfect good breeding!"

"He is also handsome, with good hair," replied Nicky, "which a young man ought likewise to be, if he possibly can. His character is thereby complete."

"I was very much flattered by his asking me for cocaine a second time. I did not expect such a compliment."

"Did not you? *I* did for you, you are known for having the best product. But that is one great difference between us. Compliments always take *you* by surprise, and *me* never. What could be more natural than his asking you again? He could not help seeing that you were about five times as slutty as every other woman in the room. No thanks to his celebrity for that. Well, he certainly is very agreeable, and I give you leave to do a line with him. You have liked many a stupider person. . . ."

"WTF, Nicky!"

"Oh! You are a great deal too apt, you know, to like people in general. You never see a fault in anybody. All the world is good and agreeable in your eyes. I never heard you speak ill of a human being in my life, except, of course, Britney . . . and maybe Lindsey . . . and that paparazzi you hit with your Bentley . . . and . . ."

"OMG. I would wish not to be hasty in censuring anyone, but I *always* tweet what I think."

"I know you do, and it is *that* which makes the wonder. With *your* good sense, to be honestly blind to the follies and nonsense of others! Affectation of candour is common enough—one-night stands are easy enough to come by. But to be candid without ostentation or design—to take the good of every hot body and make it still hotter by your association, and say nothing of the bad—belongs to you alone. And so, you like this guy's friends, too, do you? Their celebrity is not equal to his."

"Hell no, not at first. But they get hotter after you converse with them. Robert Pattinson is to live with Justin and keep the party going at his house, and I am much mistaken if we shall not find him a very charming neighbor in the Hollywood Hills."

Nicky listened in silence while texting her BFF, but was not convinced. Their behaviour at the Halloween bash had not been calculated to please in general, and with more quickness of observation and less ditziness than her sister, she was very little disposed to approve of these dudes. They were, in fact, very fine talents, not deficient in good humour when they were pleased, nor in the power of being agreeable where they chose it; but proud and conceited. They were rather handsome, had been educated by Disney, had a fortune to rival her Hilton inheritance, were in the habit of spending more than they ought and of associating with people of rank, and were therefore in every respect entitled to think well of themselves, and meanly of others. Pattinson was at least of a respectable family in the north of England, a circumstance more deeply impressed on their memories than Bieber's fortune, which had been acquired mostly due to a haircut.

PART 3

Superheroes, Vampires, and Pemberley, Oh, My!

Could there be anything more entertaining than Darcy as a vampire? We didn't think so. Of the entries in the Bad Austen contest, many of them were mashups of some of our favorite novels, television shows, and movies. Yes, we mean *Star Wars*. Read on for some Austen-esque stories that are the result of two very different worlds colliding.

⟶ Bedside Manners ⟵
C. MOORE

"Any half-wit can see that she's set her cap on Chase," remarked the physician, "though I cannot see why. He's a pretty pink, to be sure, but exceedingly vain."

"You're just jealous," said his colleague. "Besides, your own sense of vanity far outstrips his."

The first physician twirled his walking stick. "Foreman, why the deuce must you persist in wearing purple cravats? You'll make our idiot patients cast up their accounts."

Foreman smiled. "A fine parry! See, I knew you were jealous."

"I do not desire Miss Cameron. She's nubile, to be sure, but gold tresses do not suit her. 'Tis Miss Cuddy whom I would fain bed." The physician glanced up as a dark-haired lady entered his study. "Aha, good day, dear Miss Cuddy! She of the shapely posterior and plunging décolletages."

Miss Cuddy lifted one perfectly shaped brow. She was far too well-bred to acknowledge such a brutish greeting. Instead, she said, "Good day, Dr. House. I have a new case for you. That is, unless you would rather earn yourself a fortnight's clinic duty?"

"Touché!" quipped Dr. House, casting a wry look at Foreman. "Do you see how this fair creature has me completely at sixes and sevens? I worship you, Miss Cuddy!"

"You worship no other but yourself, sir. Now here is the file."

Dr. House took up said document and gave it a cursory perusal. As Miss Cuddy moved to withdraw, he beckoned her back. "Tell me, my adored one, have you yet restored my steed to his rightful place in the stables?"

Miss Cuddy sighed. "Your request was denied. There is another for whom walking further would be a still greater burden. You and I both know your alleged war injury was in fact sustained during a horserace."

"Racing, ay! Racing into battle!" objected House. "I earned a medal for that."

"You earned a fine purse, though you were dragged the last ten yards by the stirrups!" chortled Foreman.

"Traitor!" snapped House, glaring. "And a liar, as well! Everyone's a liar in this dashed place!"

Miss Cuddy smiled knowingly and exited without another word.

Dr. House stewed in silence for a minute. Then he seized a quill, scratched out a quick note, and rang for the messenger.

"What shall you do now?" wondered Dr. Foreman.

"I'll come up with a plan," growled House, "just as soon as Wilson brings me a fresh bottle of laudanum!"

DID YOU KNOW?

Many people who haven't actually read Jane Austen have an idea of her as a prim and proper writer of ladylike prose, or perhaps a writer of extravagant Regency romances. A reading of her novels, with their sharp, dry wit, splendid nonsense, and intricate exploration of the psychological truths behind human behavior, will completely explode these mistaken notions. However, even many of her most passionate fans have no idea how very far from "prim and proper" she can be. Austen's letters are quite revealing in that regard, but the most illuminating evidence of her writerly interest in the vicious, violent, stupid, and silly (more to the taste of raucous boys than refined ladies) can be found in the juvenilia.

Jack & Alice, written when Jane was in her early teens and dedicated to her brother Frank, then away at sea serving in the navy, contains an exuberantly drawn cast of flawed characters: "The Johnsons were a family of Love, & though a little addicted to the Bottle & the Dice, had many good Qualities."

The character Alice "almost came to Blows" against Lady Williams in one well-lubricated rage. Drunkenness was certainly very common at the time but is very little touched upon in Austen's later work—and certainly not among women! Violence is relished, too: The lovely Lucy is caught in a man-trap and then poisoned by a rival who is herself hanged for the offense. And it is all rollicking fun.

⌐ Gone with the Pride ⌐
SANDRA LONG

That a recent widower in possession of children must be in need of a wife was a belief held so strongly by Scarlett that she presumed Ashley would be her next of kin.

"Ashley, I have pined for the loss of your affections, but you are now free to make me an offer."

"You have misunderstood. I cannot marry you."

The lady was without speech; it was unfathomable to her that a woman could be refused an offer of marriage.

Ashley observed an unusual lack of discourse and so, with a sense of propriety, quickly filled the void. "Indeed you are mistaken of my desires. My inclinations are not toward ladies."

"Don't trifle with me, Ashley. No ladies? Surely you don't mean you have affection only for commoners?"

More contrary the truth could be not. "Scarlett, forgive me for being forthright: Feminine pulchritude does not sail my ship."

"Oh no! You mean you are . . . unusual? How can this be? You made known no such unusualness to me."

"Pink ruffled shirts?" A lady in possession of a sharper mind might have deduced the obvious, he surmised.

Scarlett knew Rhett had a multitude of ruffles in his closet yet had no inclination to join the crew of Ashley's ship. "Shame on you! Why did not you make this clear to me before? I can't believe I have wasted my life waiting for you. You have injured me. Badly done, Ashley. . . . But are you truly firm in the certainty of your mind on this topic? Surely you could be swayed by the true love of a Southern Lady?"

At this point of time, his inclinations were fixed and nothing forthcoming from Scarlett could affect change. "Alas, it is so. But now my current circumstance has given me leave to visit my true desires. Gossip has been spreading that Rhett may be departing your company. I have taken notice of his ruffles, though pink they are not, and I am on my way to see if an attachment is a possibility between us."

"NO!!! It cannot be. Your declaration has made me mind my own heart. I think I may be in love with Rhett. I may have loved him all along. No! You cannot have him. I love Rhett! I must leave for Tara with haste. I cannot fret on this for a fortnight."

"I am sorry to have vexed you. Calm your nerves. Sit a while before you depart. Have some cold meats."

"I am not in need of sitting. I want to walk."

"Walk? It's nearly a half-mile to Tara. And in all this heat."

"I will walk. I pledge to God I shall never sit again until I reach Tara. I am most exceedingly obliged to you, Ashley. Please accept my wishes for your health and happiness, but I must be off to Tara to tell Rhett I love him."

Scarlett was as surprised as anyone to hear this proclamation. The working of her heart had been hardened by the business of maintaining Tara, but Tara now seemed a mere pile of bricks and wood that was tumbling down while her heart, a real woman's heart, was building up.

"Rhett, where are you? I walked a half-mile in the sun without a parasol to see you, and I would have walked a mile entire, just to tell you my feelings for you have changed. I am embarrassed to think what I said before, but now I know what I feel in my heart. You are the most amiable associate of my alliances.

Please tell me I am not too late. Do I still have a chance to win you back?"

Rhett descended the lengthy staircase, which was quite suitable to the position of a gentleman and by no means lacking in good taste. "Why Scarlett, I am all astonishment. But are you unwell?"

"No, I assure you I am in complete wellness. Is there truth that you are quitting my company?"

"It was my plan before you had arrived. I was prepared to tell you, by George I could care not a wit, but now I find my feelings are quite reversed. Your manners, on closer acquaintance, have improved. Could this be a dream, my darling Scarlett?"

"No, I am sure I am awake. But let us put a test to that theory."

Rhett grasped Scarlett's not unsmall waist. His back arched as he bowed down toward her pouty red mouth. The moment until their lips met seemed an eternity; indeed a flock of birds could have passed in the space between until they finally consummated the kiss. It was a dream of a kiss, but it was not a dream. Awake they were, and would be thus all night to the consternation of the neighbors.

DID YOU KNOW?

With the success of *Sense and Sensibility*, the publisher was certainly interested in Jane Austen's next novel. In revising *First Impressions*, the novel she had begun in 1796, which her father had unsuccessfully tried to have published, Jane made the manuscript quite a bit shorter than the version Mr. Austen had sent to Thomas Cadell. Thomas Egerton offered £110 for the novel she now called *Pride and Prejudice*, and although Jane had hoped for more, she accepted his offer, apparently to save Henry (and Eliza) from having to advance money again. *Pride and Prejudice* was published in January of 1813.

The reviews and general public response to this new novel were even more enthusiastic than they had been for *Sense and Sensibility*. Once again, Austen could enjoy the direct praise of only a few people because this book, too, was published anonymously, "by the Author of *Sense and Sensibility*." In those days, ladies did not seek to draw public attention to themselves. Rather than basking in the limelight of successful authorship, Jane was quietly living in the Hampshire countryside. After the publication of the book Jane so lovingly—and rightly—referred to as "my own darling Child," she and Mrs. Austen took turns reading from it to their neighbor, a poor spinster named Miss Benn. What an extraordinary picture that must have made, and all the more amusing because Miss Benn—also kept in the dark about Jane's secret—did not know she was in the presence of the author!

Woman of Wonder
SHANNON WINSLOW

No one who had ever seen Wonder Woman in her infancy would have supposed her born to be a heroine. Her character, situation, and temper were all equally against such an eventuality. And fate seemed at first wholly disinclined to lend a hand.

A glimpse of little Diana—for so she was then called—surely conjured up no image of future greatness in the beholder's eye. Indeed, as Amazons go, her looks did not exceed the average by a single jot. A graceless figure, an awkward fashion sense, and a total want of complexion combined to ill effect. The resulting picture all but shouted that this child was destined for mediocrity.

Equally unpropitious for heroism seemed the turn of little Diana's mind. She greatly preferred reading to the more standard juvenile pursuits—swordplay, mastering the lasso, fending off lightning bolts—and rarely attended to the insinuations of her well-intentioned relations that she would be wise to cultivate whatsoever latent superpowers she might possess.

Such were Diana's youthful propensities. But when a young lady is to be a heroine, the perverseness of every disobliging circumstance imaginable cannot prevent her. Something must and will happen to throw a call to heroism in her way.

By and by, her looks improved tolerably, and her other abilities developed apace to the point that her marshal arts master went so far as to call her efforts "satisfactory." Then, on the day of her eighteenth birthday, she cast a most auspicious gaze across the mystical veil that hung betwixt her home on the island of Themiscyra and the sphere of Man. Diana happened to spy there a handsome mortal of a more than usually interesting aspect, whom she thereafter made the subject of her constant study.

During a mandatory warrior-training class one day, she confided her observations to her best friend, Anita, who is also known as Power Girl. "He is just what a young man ought to be," Diana said, deftly evading the saber thrust of her male sparing partner. "Tall—a singular virtue to which every young man must by all means aspire—and I never saw such a happy union of noble character and physical perfection. Certainly, I've not encountered his equal in this place," she said with a disdainful glare at the feeble specimen cowering at the point of her sword.

"Then I give you leave to like him . . . from afar, that is," replied Anita, registering a hit against her opponent as well. "I daresay this man of yours may be possessed of a little more wit than the rest, but mortals are by nature stupid and helpless creatures."

"What care I for such trifles? I simply must be near him; nothing else will do."

"Do not be rash, Diana! As you well know, the only way for one of us to cross over to the human world is in the guise of a superhero."

"Then my course is clear."

And thus, Wonder Woman came into being.

Did You Know?

Jane fainted at news of her family's move to Bath, tradition has it, not only because she very much loved Steventon—the only home she'd ever known—but also because she hated Bath—and, indeed, cities in general. Critics and biographers have turned to the letters Jane wrote while she was anticipating the move and detected that she was putting on a good front but was in fact very unhappy.

Jane describes Bath in a letter as "vapour, shadow, smoke & confusion," which does not sound as if she liked the place very much. Her other letters from the first weeks in Bath are also rather depressed-sounding. "I cannot anyhow continue to find people agreeable," she writes rather hopelessly to Cassandra. Jane attends social gatherings and gives reports of them that are either complaints about their disagreeableness or sharp-edged jokes about those present. There is little evidence that she was finding life in Bath very enjoyable at the beginning of her stay there.

In *Northanger Abbey*, Catherine Morland finds it a delightful place, astonishing in the variety of people and activities it offers, especially when compared with the sleepy country village she has come from. As Mrs. Allen inimitably puts it, "it is just the place for young people—and indeed for every body else too." Catherine more sensibly, if naively, exclaims, "Oh! who can ever be tired of Bath?" Henry Tilney's answer to her probably rhetorical question may hold the key to evaluating Bath's general pleasantness or unpleasantness: "Not those who bring such fresh feelings of every sort to it, as you do." In other words, Catherine "was come to be happy," and thus Bath made her so. Did Jane Austen come there to be happy herself?

⤳ Twilight at Northanger ⤲
ANNE GLOVER

Inheritance is not always a boon. A penchant for too many cakes, the propensity to freckle under the slightest provocation of sun, and the habit of being a spendthrift were all traits one might inherit. The discovery of such inheritance was seldom as grave as the reading of a will; the recognition of such a family trait was realized when in connection with conflict.

Cathy Morland, nee Tilney's youngest sister, Jane, had inherited her dusty old collection of novels and along with it a great passion for the macabre. Like Catherine, Jane was wont to spend a whole day idle with a book ignoring her daily tasks and exasperating poor Mrs. Morland who, in her advancing years, had little more patience for a whimsical girl.

It was so that when Catherine's letter came announcing the demise of Captain Wentworth and Mr. Tilney's sudden inheritance of Northanger Abbey, her pleas for a spare sister to be sent in assistance of the great move was a welcome relief to the beleaguered Mrs. Morland.

Jane was bundled into Mr. Tilney's carriage, sent after the receipt of Mrs. Morland's response, on a brisk March morning. The journey was not overlong so that the Tilneys had sent Coachman and a groom to protect the young traveler.

Thrilled beyond anticipation, Jane tucked herself against the squabs and into a deliciously ghoulish novel.

Enraptured by the terrifying tale, Jane did not even notice when the carriage came to an abrupt halt.

It took moments before she looked up, finally noticing that the comfortable pace had ceased.

"Hello?" she called. The only answer was silence.

Jane set her book aside and slid toward the window. "Hello?" She asked again, her voice meek and a little afraid. The silence was deafening.

Craning her neck out of the open window, she looked both ways and saw nothing but a green thickness of trees.

Like an apparition appearing from thin air, a pale face was suddenly in front of her. Jane gasped, and with her hand on the carriage latch, fell forward and tumbled out of the carriage.

Suddenly strong, muscular arms were grasping and holding her.

Jane blinked and stared up into topaz eyes. Shocked beyond speech, Jane was hypnotized by the face staring down at her.

He was pale, almost sparkling, and cold to the touch. Impossibly handsome, like something out of a dream, the boy who couldn't have been more than ten and eight looked more of a man than Jane had ever seen before.

Without warning, he released an arm beneath her, allowing her feet to come crashing to the ground.

"Who are you?" she murmured.

"Are you alright, miss?" he persisted harshly in a musical voice. It was as if the heavens had opened up and the angels were singing, the sound coming from his mouth was so beautiful.

Jane gasped as she realized his eyes were changing color. The brightest spot in his flawless, dazzling cold face, they had somehow turned to a shallow green.

"What are you doing here?" she continued. "Where is everyone else?" Jane whispered. His icy fingers were suddenly wrapped around her wrists.

Without warning, the boy-man was lifting her into the carriage and closing the door behind her. He uttered a low oath before stalking toward the front of the carriage.

And almost as if awaking startled from a dream, Jane jerked back as the carriage began to move.

"Who are you?" she cried, her hand still icy from his touch now opening upon her heated cheek.

The sight of Northanger Abbey at twilight looming in the distance was mystical and menacing. Jane squirmed uncomfortably in her seat, willing the journey to be over, as she looked out the carriage window once more. She had hoped to catch view of the mysterious stranger again, now wondering if it wasn't a dream.

When the carriage finally came to a slow roll in front of the large stone building, Jane blew out a sigh of exhausted relief.

Shortly, she was gathered into her sister's waiting arms. "Jane, how glad I am to see you," Catherine exclaimed as her arm went around her sister's shoulder.

"Cathy, the strangest thing has happened."

Catherine raised an eyebrow in anticipation.

"The carriage was stopped by this boy—this man. His eyes changed color and he was so cold to the touch. . . ." Jane's voice trailed off in wonder.

"Jane, do you like scary stories?" Catherine asked, helping her sister up the steps of Northanger.

Jane nodded dully.

"Then I will tell you about him. But only if you promise never to go near him again."

DID YOU KNOW?

It does not appear that Jane Austen pursued publication of *Lady Susan*, her completed novel in letters. Rather, we have her nephew, James-Edward Austen-Leigh, to thank for its publication. He included the text, taken from an untitled manuscript transcribed in 1805 (a "fair copy"), in the second edition of his *Memoir of Jane Austen*, published in 1871. It is a fascinating work from Austen's early period, probably written between 1793 and 1795. The consistently high emotion and the melodramatic events and speech in *Lady Susan* also mark it as an early work.

There is none of Austen's brilliant re-creation of the ordinary and everyday, which is everywhere in the later novels. It is, however, an astonishingly impressive work for any writer, never mind a girl not yet twenty years old.

Austen's bad mothers in the major novels are mainly guilty of neglect and foolishness, but Lady Susan is downright wicked in her treatment of her daughter Frederica, whom she is determined to marry off very much against her will. This wickedness is also shown in Lady Susan's cool, remorseless indulgence in adultery and her manipulation of others for her own convenience. However, she is also dazzlingly attractive to men and to many women—beautiful, strong-willed, witty, spirited, unsentimental (some of which traits are usefully hidden when necessary under a sweet, gentle exterior).

Lady Susan is, as many readers have noted, a kind of immoral version of Austen's witty, spirited heroines Elizabeth Bennet and Emma Woodhouse—and perhaps, even more, of the endlessly debated figure of Mary Crawford from *Mansfield Park*. Just as she does in the case of the winning Miss Crawford, however, Austen makes her disapproval of Lady Susan clear when she has that character say, "I take town in my way to that insupportable spot, a country village." Austen loved the country, and those characters in her novels who do not like it and prefer the "town"—London—must ·and do have the wrong values.

⤳ The Bennet Bunch ⤳
EILEEN MITCHELL

It is a whimsically acknowledged truth that Mrs. Bennet was a lovely lady who was bringing up five very lovely girls. Some of them had hair of gold like their mother, the youngest one, Lydia, bedecked in curls.

Coincidentally, through fortuitous proximity, there was a man named Bingley, dispatched from London with five sisters of his own. They were six siblings sojourning all together, yet they were much alone.

Till the one day when the Bennets met the Bingleys, and they surmised that it was much more than a hunch that this assemblage must somehow intermingle, if not at tea, if not in town, perhaps at lunch.

But before even a few lines of formal invitation had been extended to the bachelor Bingley, Mr. Bennet announced his intentions to throw in a good word for his daughter Lizzy, much to the consternation of his wife.

"Lizzy, Lizzy, Lizzy!" Mrs. Bennet exclaimed, quite disconcerted. "We have five daughters with much to recommend them. Why must you always give Lizzy the preference? Her sister Jane is twice as handsome."

"Much to recommend them?" Mr. Bennet parried with his usual endearing, misogynistic charm. "Jane is handsome, indeed, with the lantern-jawed profile of a longshoreman. Kitty is an inconsiderate consumptive whose hacking disturbs my revelry.

Lydia is a glandular case of freakish height, suitable for employment in a traveling circus, and that other daughter—her name escapes me at the moment—scarcely makes a memorable impression. At least Lizzy has a quickness about her."

Lizzy, Lizzy, Lizzy! Jane echoed her mother's protest in silent pique. Her father's effusiveness toward Elizabeth was a source of constant vexation, thereby inspiring Jane to concoct a plan. She would outshine Lizzy on the croquet field, and then perhaps her father would admire her cleverness and Mr. Bingley would favor her hand in marriage. For she had overheard, through closed doors, that there was nothing a gentleman fancied more than a quick girl who knew how to handle a mallet.

Within a fortnight, an invitation to luncheon had been dispatched to Mr. Bingley. He first declined and then capitulated at the urging of his friend Mr. Darcy, who extracted an invitation when he learned croquet was on the agenda. It was not so much Mr. Darcy's love of the game, but rather his supercilious delight in watching the designing females comically entangled in stakes and hoops, and felled by mallets. Nothing like a good stumble to brighten his day. How his eyes sparkled with pleasure at their feminine posturings on the manicured lawns, never more so than when an errant swing upended a player. His inability to stifle merriment at such moments often turned the tide of his popularity, despite his good looks.

When the day of the party arrived, Mrs. Bennet's nerves were jangling like porcelain marionettes. Vexed from the preparations, she forthwith instructed her servant, Alice, to attend to the remaining details: drawing up the menu, going to market, slaughtering the ox, polishing the silver, assembling the croquet field, and renovating the manor. Enervated at the sight of her servant's exertions, Mrs. Bennet took to her bed. Amidst fluffing Mrs. Bennet's pillows and turning the roast, Alice was kept exceedingly busy attending to the ox.

When at length the guests arrived and were assembled on the lawn, a healthy rivalry ensued among the ladies to capture the attention of the eligible gentlemen. Those left standing after the melee were entreated to play croquet. Jane seized the moment to make a favorable impression on Mr. Bingley by driving the croquet mallet with such vigor as to send the ball flying into the air.

"My nose!" cried Lizzy, upon being struck in the face by her sister's misguided enthusiasm, not to mention the wooden missile that had once been a croquet ball.

If Jane's ambition was to outdo the others, she succeeded handsomely as Mr. Bingley was indeed impressed by her unmatched boldness with the mallet, Lizzy's maiming notwithstanding. The question of whether the shot was mere gusto or repressed envy would never be answered, but Mr. Bingley was nonetheless captivated by the rather unconventional display of coquetry.

Elizabeth made a full recovery and harbored no ill will toward Jane in the event that Mr. Darcy's attentions were drawn to her over the mishap. Where he had once overlooked her entirely for what he considered her ordinariness, he later reconsidered, not coincidentally, after a misplaced guffaw at her misshapen countenance threatened his reputation in town. Encouraged by Bingley to call upon her with roses, a full-blown courtship took flower along with the bouquet.

The bloodlines, that day, were destined to comingle, ultimately inspiring a saucy jingle: The possibilities were pregnant at lunch, and that's the way they all became the Bennet bunch.

DID YOU KNOW?

When she was just sixteen, Austen wrote a brilliantly funny "unfinished Novel in Letters" called *Lesley Castle*, this time dedicating her work to her brother Henry. Here we can see the beginnings of one of her comic specialties, the monomaniacal talker who thinks of the world as it relates to just one subject and turns all events and all discussions back to the one thing dearest her heart. Mrs. Allen, from *Northanger Abbey*, with her obsession with clothes, is the finest example of this type in the novels. Like *Jack & Alice*, *Lesley Castle* also contains some improper matter for a young girl (never mind a clergyman's daughter) to be writing about—for example, adultery and child abandonment go unpunished.

⌒ Dead and Loving It ⌒
CATHY TAVERNIER

Mr. Charles Bingley and Mr. Fitzwilliam Darcy were both dead, but they had not given in to discouragement. Rather, they made for themselves a remarkable posthumous life that included many of the same entertainments they enjoyed while living: eating, drinking—as they particularly needed to drink still—and courting young ladies—this, too, being a pastime as much required as it remained pleasurable. It rarely occurred to them to bemoan their glorious past lives; for being deceased, while liberating in several ways, also allotted them many similar experiences they had grown accustomed to while living.

"What am I to make of this ball to which we are heading, Darcy?" asked Mr. Bingley one fine spring evening. He trotted down a dirt path upon his black horse beside his fellow mounted partner.

"It is the perfect scenario for us," replied Mr. Darcy, unusually interested in this ball, despite not being fond of them in general. "I have it on good authority that hardly an eligible man—nary a card-playing group of old chaps— is in attendance. We would be fools for passing on such a unique opportunity."

"That is capital, indeed! Well done, Darcy. We shall dine finely this evening," said Mr. Bingley, pulling down the brim of his hat. He felt relief, for he recalled recent dances he and Mr. Darcy had attended, uninvited, with a fair amount of gentlemen present. Unfortunately, as a result, drastic measures to purge them from the engagements by those overseeing men were undertaken. If anything, this evening would prove significantly easier for the two of them to retain their persons amongst the ladies present.

Moments later, they dismounted from their steeds. Much noise and merry-making escaped outside the windows of the large manor, and, as Mr. Darcy had been informed, there certainly stood mainly fine young maidens laughing and chattering inside.

"As I said earlier, hardly a man to be seen," repeated Mr. Darcy after peering in through a foggy window. Mr. Bingley could not help but quicken his step as they approached the entrance. He was glad he wore his favorite blue coat! As soon as the two stepped inside, all the prattle and racket ceased, replaced by gasps and awestruck expressions.

With all the attention immediately diverted to the two, Darcy grabbed the lapels of his coat and flapped out his elbows. "Good evening, young ladies without gentlemen! We are lords of the finest social order of the Undead, and we have come here to suck your blood," announced he, bowing with all formalities. Two distinctive fangs hung out over his lower lip for all to see.

"And, to drink it, as well!" added Mr. Bingley, bowing and exposing his own fangs also, but sporting a happy smile.

"Va-vampires!" screamed a young girl, pointing in their direction, as if it were necessary. Suddenly, the room erupted into a cacophony of yelps and shrieks. Yet something about the tone seemed oddly untainted by fear.

"They are so . . . handsome!" shouted another young woman, whipping a fan in front of her face. The excitement of the maiden crowd grew higher, as expected, but not more fearful.

"Suck my blood, vampires!" shouted a few ladies in a synchronized fashion, as they all dashed at the two men-of-the-moment. "No! Not hers! Mine! You may drink as much of my blood as you wish, good sirs!" Such were the commands howled by the animated crowd, as they tore off shawls and craned their necks to the side to ease the two vampires' imbibing.

"How very courteous of you all," remarked Mr. Bingley over the roaring cluster of maidens, as they stepped and trounced on one another to draw near him.

"This is the way, is it not?" asked an uncertain, shy girl, directing her unveiled ivory neck at Mr. Bingley.

"Why, yes, that is the correct position we vampires require when feeding," he assured her. His delight grew more fervent with each exposed limb shoved within his vicinity.

"You see, Bingley," began Mr. Darcy, "we may have been dead for a time, but, as is quite evident, we are as popular as ever." A handful of women swarmed him all at once as he nearly winked at Mr. Bingley.

"I will drink to that. I dare say we were never quite this popular before! And, let it not be said that Darcy and Bingley went out of this world without leaving an impression of some sort, including the kind we make upon the maiden neck!" shouted Bingley, as he bit ardently into one such eager neck.

And, thus, the grand feast ensued for the evening, as the two deceased—yet, still undoubtedly popular—young men drank the crimson fluid to their hearts' content.

Did You Know?

In May of 1779 the third Austen boy, Edward, was twelve years old. Thomas Knight, a distant Austen cousin (and the landlord of Steventon), visited the parsonage with his new wife, Catherine. Apparently they became so fond of Edward that they asked permission to take him with them as they continued their "honeymoon" travels. This seems to have been the beginning of their extraordinary attachment to the boy, which culminated in their actually adopting him a few years later. The Knights were very wealthy, and since they were also childless, Edward stood to inherit their fortune, including several large estates.

Once again, this may seem to show a cold-heartedness toward their children on the part of the Austens—another chance to give them away as they did when they sent them as infants to foster families in the village—but the truth is that the adoption scheme was a great success in every way. The Knights were not only wealthy, but good. Jane was very fond of Mrs. Knight, who was actually the writer's only patron, giving her some kind of annual allowance. And Edward remained very close to the Austen family throughout his life. We may have Mrs. Knight to thank for Jane Austen's novels on much stronger grounds than her bestowal of the "usual Fee" on Jane, for it was Edward's inheritance that ultimately supplied Jane with the comfort and security of the house in which she wrote and/or revised her novels: Chawton Cottage, one of the world's greatest literary landmarks.

Jersey Shore Does Brighton
(or, If Jane Scripted Jersey Shore)
SHELLEY RUSSELL

We find our friends of questionable rank on holiday at Brighton. Alas, this holiday is of little distinction from past seasons, with many members of the group frequently casting up their accounts as the girls prove again quite able to elevate their demimonde status whilst frequently imbibing body shots and other libations at the local pub and inspiring frequent displays of swordplay amongst the local rakes.

"Oh, what a wonderful welcome we have received. I presented myself at a fine establishment on the evening of late. To be sure, I shall find my perfect gorilla in the UK." Snooki had ensured that her signature poof was of greatest proportion prior to her introductions the evening before.

"My dear Snooki, I pray you find me not indelicate to your feelings, as I am compelled to converse with you on a matter most sensitive to your good, if not questionable name," began J Woww. (You are familiar with J Woww, the irascible chit whose own moniker aptly denotes her more than ample and artificial décolletage?)

"Surely, you mean not to refer to the kindly escort provided to me by the gentle constable who transported me to the pokey on the Jersey Shore. He afforded me every consolation and comfort following the faint I succumbed to, which found my visage planted in the sand."

"To be sure, it is the continuance of your lack of prudence that lays fear upon my soul. I find it necessary to confer upon you a matter in need of your most urgent attentions. I shall speak plainly, dear Snooks, that you find yourself too often, too far in your cups."

Sensing the demise of the well-intentioned advice afforded by J Woww, the paternal "The Situation" deems it prudent to speak his mind and devise some sense of order. "The concerns you share for Snooki may well be deferred by way of GTL (Gym, Tan, Laundry) as it always returns me to an affable condition. Come, ladies. Let us trifle no more over these matters, which, to be sure, affect us all."

Considering the weakened pallor experienced by even less sunshine than the Jersey Shore can afford, the girls concede and the happy party departs. Once again, a tragic consequence has been averted by "The Situation."

The Weasleys Visit Netherfield Park
KIMHPARK

"Did you get it? Did you pick up the dance tonic like I asked you to?"

"Yeah, I got it," moaned Ron, showing Hermione the bottle he picked up from the apothecary. "But must we do this, Hermione?"

"Oh, stop grousing. You promised. You can't back out on me now. Besides, I've already bewitched the book to make space for us in the story, and we mustn't keep the pages waiting."

"Yes, but I didn't realize it would be a Jane Austen story. I thought it would be a Buffy, the Vampire Slayer. You know, something with a little rough and tumble? Remember last week? Wasn't that fun?"

Hermione glared at Ron, folding her arms across her chest. Ron looked down at his shoes. "How 'bout a nice dinner out?" he tried. "Wouldn't that suffice?"

"No, a dinner out would not suffice, Ronald. It's our first wedding anniversary, and I want it to be elegant. I want to dance with you at Netherfield Park, alongside Elizabeth Bennet and Fitzwilliam Darcy. Now put your jacket on, please. It's time to apparate."

Ron shrugged into his dinner jacket. Hermione took Ron's hand in hers, tapped her worn copy of *Pride and Prejudice* with her wand, and pop! the two of them vanished into the pages of Austen's nineteenth-century England. The neigh of horses, crunching of carriage wheels on gravel, and giddy salutations of the arriving guests echoed across the lawn to where the pair stood under the trees, taking in the scene. They had a good view of the great house—its windows thrown wide, tapestries pulled elegantly aside, and servants making the rounds with silver trays of champagne and hors d'oeuvres.

"Oh, isn't it lovely?" said Hermione. Ron frowned. *It might be*, he thought, *once I get a hold of those choice meats and cheeses*. Ron and Hermione made their way through the arriving guests and into the great hall. Ron grabbed two glasses of champagne, swallowed the first in one gulp and poured his dance tonic into the second. He was just about to put the second to his lips and swallow when Hermione gasped and grabbed his arm, "Oh, Ron! It's Elizabeth Bennet! See? In the ivory gown? And look! Mr. Darcy is applying for her hand to dance. See how she's caught off-guard by his request and says yes without really thinking it through?"

"Uh huh. That's nice," said Ron, stepping in front of a servant passing with an hors d'oeuvres tray. Ron put his full glass in the middle of the tray and proceeded to gobble up the sweets surrounding it. The attendant stood holding the tray, waiting, eyes bulging, for Ron to pause for breath; the poor man had never seen anyone take such liberties with the meats and cheeses.

"Oh look! Here comes Mr. Darcy!" said Hermione. Fitzwilliam Darcy glided toward them, and seeing the full glass of champagne on the now-empty hors d'oeuvres tray, he promptly picked it up and drank it down. Ron frowned and gulped.

"Let's go," said Hermione. "The dance will be starting soon, and I want to be as near to Lizzie and Darcy as possible." The dancers took their places on the floor in two long lines across from each other. Ron stood next to Darcy, the man himself, who appeared to be no worse for wear from consuming the tonic. *That's good*, thought Ron. *I didn't want to drink that stuff anyway. That witch may have given me a dud for all I know.*

No sooner had Ron finished this thought than the musicians began playing and Mr. Darcy skidded across the floor on his knees, turned a somersault, and spun on his head. No one else moved.

Jaws dropped wide as Mr. Darcy grabbed his partner around the waist and spun the unsuspecting damsel across the floor with a flourish and pomp unlike anything Hertfordshire had as yet seen. Ron watched in shock. Hermione's eyes bulged. Stealthily, she withdrew her wand from her handbag, preparing to fix the situation when most unexpectedly Darcy threw Elizabeth into a low dip, and the crowd applauded uproariously. The dancing partners blushed and bowed and then withdrew from each other.

"Lizzie, what have you done to poor Mr. Darcy?" asked Charlotte Lucas.

"I have no idea," replied Lizzie, who looked after Mr. Darcy with more earnest intrigue than the story should have allowed at this point.

Hermione turned a suspicious eye on Ron. "What did you do?" she asked.

"Nothing. Honestly. You know, there's really no accounting for how English gentry will behave."

"Yes," grinned Hermione, brushing away the last stray bits of meat and cheese crumbs from Ron's lapel. "No accounting, indeed."

DID YOU KNOW?

With all her intellectual sophistication and a satirical wit that would have shone in the most urbane of London salons, and despite the pleasure she found in visiting London and other cities, Jane Austen was at heart a country girl. She deeply loved the

Hampshire countryside where she grew up, and she was overjoyed to return to the country once again in later life. Like her heroines, she was a great walker, and country walking is much more pleasant exercise than city walking—at least when the roads are dry. When the roads were wet, the Austen girls wore pattens—inelegant but practical overshoes designed to keep the feet dry on sloppy roads. Austen's pleasure in this activity calls to mind *Pride and Prejudice*, in which Elizabeth Bennet, another witty country girl, walks alone to Netherfield, "jumping over stiles and springing over puddles with impatient activity, and finding herself at last within view of the house, with weary ancles, dirty stockings, and a face glowing with the warmth of exercise."

⌁ Mr. Collins (Part I) ⌁
TAMI ABSI

Elizabeth invited Charlotte on a walk around her family's estate.

"Elizabeth, you mustn't scold me," Charlotte whined. "I am twenty-seven and fear spinsterhood."

"Oh, my dear," Elizabeth replied, "how could you marry Mr. Collins? Never has a man possessed such a countenance. His jowls grew as a scaffold to sustain his overly large, square, turned-up nose, and the jowls continue in the endeavor."

"I must remind you," Charlotte said, "he owns your family's estate; it is legally his as your eldest male cousin. You choose to insult him; though, he has no inclination to greedily turn the seven of you out in the streets. He only wishes to provide and care for you. In return . . ." Charlotte's voice trailed off.

"My reason for alarm is sound, I assure you. His demeanor makes my blood run cold. When he came to our house a month ago, he ate nothing. He talked with pomposity through the dinner, and he stared at each and every one of my sister's necks," Elizabeth said.

"Necks or necklines?" Charlotte questioned.

"Oh, I respect him as a minister. I must say I meant necks, not bodices."

"Odd," Charlotte said, crossing her arms over her chest. "He was drawn to my general neck area the other night, and his demeanor changed."

"When?" Elizabeth asked.

Charlotte scurried along with Elizabeth's long strides and spoke between gasps. "Let me remember. Yes, the moon was large and low; it was the night of the full harvest moon. He began to inhale around my neck, not like a man enjoying a scent, but like a dog hungering after meat. When I questioned him, he claimed to be fasting, and the lack of food had made him lightheaded."

"How long does he fast?" Charlotte continued. "In his whole life, and even as a child, have you seen your cousin eat?"

"No," Elizabeth stated. "No, now that I think of it, I haven't. Never have I thought much on the matter—why he makes me feel as he does. Neither have I seen him eat nor has my father allowed him access our pigs. Recently, when he came to dine, Father directed our servants on the matter saying it wouldn't be wise to allow Mr. Collins in the barn."

Charlotte and Elizabeth had arrived at the barn. Leaning on the fence rails, they both considered the pigs in the pen. Charlotte said, "What harm could he do the pigs?"

"I recall when we were children and Mr. Collins was not yet in knickers, Mr. Collins and his father, my uncle, came to visit. My father found one of our suckling piglets dead, and Father blamed my cousin. It was the last time they visited during my uncle's life."

"How could a very young child battle a 350-pound sow to gain access to a piglet? The sows are fierce when protecting their young," Charlotte said.

With the sun waning, Elizabeth shivered a bit, and after suggesting they return home to the hearth, she said, "Charlotte, I know the wedding is three months away. Please come and stay with us for a time before the wedding. Mr. Collins is generous in his visitations throughout the rectory. We expect to see him often, and if you stayed here, he could call on you in an appropriate manner without raising gossip."

Charlotte accepted the invitation to stay with Elizabeth Bennet and her family. Soon after her arrival, a screech wafted from the barn. Mr. Bennet remarked, "Sounds as if a servant discovered something amiss."

Mr. Bennet threw a cape about his shoulders and had almost arrived at the barn with Elizabeth and Charlotte scurrying behind, working against the wind to both sprint and tie bonnet strings in the same moments.

The servant woman ran from the pigpens and shouted to Mr. Bennet, "Oh, dear sir, what sort of minister is Mr. Collins? Has Lady Catherine misunderstood the man's calling?"

On the ground, in the pen, a dead piglet lay. The sow rested while feeding her young, and amidst the piglets Mr. Collins lay. He drank heartily, attached to one teat. He raised one finger, dripping in mud, to direct whoever stood behind him to wait, for he showed no inclination to rise and bow properly.

Charlotte fainted, and fortunately, Mr. Bennet caught her. Mr. Bennet shook his head as he murmured to Elizabeth, "This I have feared for years. Mr. Collins longs for a child, and I fear if he has his way, the child will have nothing to eat. His mother did her best, giving him suck for years and hiring wet nurses thereafter. Now, his diseased desires have brought him again to this."

Elizabeth watched Mr. Collins's legs twitch with delight in the mud. "I am not unashamed," she exclaimed.

⌁ Mr. Collins (Part 2) ⌁
TAMI ABSI

The next day, Mrs. Bennet spent the remainder of the day soundly in bed. Her remonstrations kept the servants too busy to attend to truly important matters. Elizabeth knew dinner would include but one course. They would probably eat common meat pie—it being all the kitchen staff could manage between their fanning and fawning over her mother.

Near dinnertime, Mrs. Bennet called for Elizabeth and Charlotte. Charlotte looked earnestly concerned, for she did not know there was no need for worry. Elizabeth, well aware her mother's nervous fits could easily be cured by a turn in events, sat at the bedside and dutifully patted her mother's hand.

Mrs. Bennet adjusted her bed cap down to cover any stray hairs. "Oh, my dear Charlotte, I am sure this news concerning your fiance has provided you with quite a shock. This event has torn my nerves apart."

Mr. Bennet had joined the trio, feigning distress for his wife. "It is my concern, my dear, that one of these days when your nerves are torn apart, they may not rejoin. Over twenty years, I have been distressed to see the puzzling apart of your nerves. I await the parlor trick to see a whole nervous system functioning once again."

Elizabeth said, "Father, teasing Mother now is not sane." She turned toward Charlotte and said, "Shall we focus on matters of greater weight? Surely, you will not marry Mr. Collins after learning he is discontent to break bread in the natural sense."

Mrs. Bennet sat upright for the first time that day. "Oh, but the wedding must go on. Should my dear nephew's instability be publically canvassed, all might be lost. Think of it. Our Lady

Catherine will take the pulpit from him. His Majesty would hear of the dishonor, and our family would lose our estates. I beg you, Charlotte; do you wish us to be without hearth and home?"

Charlotte leaned forward and glanced at both women, but then rested her eyes out the window toward the copse. "No, nor do I wish to be without."

Elizabeth alighted from her chair and stood in front of the window, thus regaining her friend's full attention. "Charlotte, how could you marry a pompous, monstrous man to whom the entire community gives respect and admiration? Would you allow your life to be a lie?"

Mrs. Bennet yanked on her bed cap, causing it to sit askew. "Mr. Bennet, please help our daughter to see that Charlotte's marriage would keep our lives tidily together; there would be no sin in it. Taking a man from his appointed pulpit should not be our doing. If God puts him there, we are doing the good Lord's work to keep him there. Don't you agree, Mr. Bennet?"

Mr. Bennet exhaled a married man's sigh. "I agree that keeping the truth from those in power gives them little ammunition to fire in our direction. Simply because one keeps the truth, one doesn't become a liar, my dear."

Charlotte took an opportunity to speak and seated herself amidst the crossfire of glares and glances. "Let me compare evils. Would it be better to marry a man like Mr. Darcy? The whole of society has recognized his narrow-minded and indecent behavior. I would marry a man respected by the whole, and for the other part, when he says that of which I might be reasonably ashamed, I can join the whole and look away. For it has been established he is respectable, though sometimes lacking the right words for a situation, but respectable. We only need to agree with him to manage his instability. He mustn't make known to the whole that which would draw indivertible attention."

Mrs. Bennet exhaled a married woman's sigh. "You only need be a good girl for the next ten years, and then you will be an old married woman, allowed a day in bed every now and then."

Elizabeth stood and only her father heard her stamp a stubborn foot beneath her skirt. "I guess it has been settled, and although I believe it to be settled poorly, the heaviest weights do sink first. Is Mr. Collins joining us for dinner to watch us eat it?" Elizabeth asked.

"My nerves will not have it, I'm afraid," Mrs. Bennet declared. "The servants have orders to bring my dinner to my bed."

Mr. Bennet arose, too, and took Elizabeth's arm. "We are not to speak of this at dinner. Now that my brother has died, only the four of us are privy to this matter, and we must keep it. Tomorrow, we will join Mr. Collins in the library for an interview. Miss Charlotte, I will enlighten you how nourishment might be provided to your husband, and we shall not speak of it again."

DID YOU KNOW?

Some readers of *Persuasion*, Austen's last completed novel, believe there is still something "incomplete" about it. It is quite a bit shorter than any of the other novels with the exception of the early *Northanger Abbey*, and the William Elliot plot thread has been seen as slightly underdeveloped. Austen started writing *The Elliots*—her working title for *Persuasion*—in 1815, and by the time she completed it, her health had begun to fail. It is possible that she wasn't able to do everything with this novel that she would have liked to do. Still, many people choose *Persuasion* as their favorite Austen novel. While no one could deny that the dazzling *Emma* was more technically brilliant, *Persuasion* is surely the most moving of Austen's novels, and that might explain its special place among them.

Jane Austen finished *Persuasion* on July 18, 1816. Or, rather, she wrote "Finis" at the end of the manuscript but then felt dissatisfied with the ending and rewrote it, discarding one chapter entirely, revising another, and adding new material. Because of this, we have two manuscript chapters—the only original manuscript pages from the finished novels.

The original ending, which is usually appended to modern editions, was first published by Jane's nephew, who included it in the second edition of his *Memoir* in 1871. As he so correctly notes, the manuscript chapters are inferior to the revision but in themselves are quite worthy pieces of writing. In them, Anne

Elliot plays a more passive role in letting Captain Wentworth know her feelings for him, which happens when she assures him she is not engaged to William Elliot. Admiral Croft has insisted that Wentworth ask about this because he wants to vacate Kellynch Hall if she and Mr. Elliot have any desire to live there before the Crofts's lease is up. But Anne is the one responsible for the original separation between herself and Wentworth, and she deeply wounded him when she broke off the engagement, so it is fitting that her words should affect their reconciliation in a more active way than this.

The revision contains wonderful new material featuring the Musgroves, and, of course, the breathtaking scene in which Anne and Captain Wentworth communicate their feelings "under cover," as it were. Anne, in a dialogue with Captain Harville, defends the constancy of women in love, declaring that men forget sooner and women love longer even when their love is hopeless. Captain Wentworth hears this and writes a letter to Anne declaring his love while he pretends to be writing to someone else. The suspense is exquisite, and the dialogue perhaps the most gripping in all of Austen's writing. With this new ending, Austen allows quiet Anne Elliot a most eloquent defense of women: "Men have had every advantage of us in telling their own story. Education has been theirs in so much higher a degree; the pen has been in their hands."

⌐ Leia: A Novel ⌐
Martti Nelson

Princess Leia Organa, lately of the space-transport The Millennium Falcon, pulled a lever in an effort to re-engage the damaged engine of that vehicle. The flying hack sat in woeful disrepair since its captain, the dastardly pirate Han Solo, piloted the rickety rust bucket into a deep crater upon a planet-like body afloat in the dark abyss of the heavens. It took all of the venerable princess' composure not to direct an improper word at the stubborn lever, which protested even after she had welded it whilst wearing a most displeasing set of goggles, unfashionable lo these past three seasons.

One moment later, Mr. Solo, who was most assuredly not a gentleman of any means, manners, or delightful expressions, ambled by in an inelegant fashion, resembling a scruffy nerfherder. In perfect bad character, he reached for the princess like a Wookiee desirous of a side of fresh bantha. His hand brushed hers, which was, at the moment, unprotected by a glove. Such familiar contact was, naturally, not befitting a royal of her dignity and stature in the universe. With a most bitter sigh, she rebuffed his efforts at chicanery, which was surely all the smuggler was about.

The villain spoke: "My most humble pardons, Your Worship. I intervened only in an effort to assist you in your welding distress."

Princess Leia rolled her expressive eyes, for the odious man declined to utilize her proper title, though she had schooled him in the use of it repeatedly at the frozen tundras of the Rebel base, located in the neighborhood of Hoth. "Mr. Solo," replied she, "kindly refrain from addressing me thusly."

"Indeed, Princess."

The maiden frowned, for his acquiescence puzzled her. She bristled with disdain for the ruffian, yet her heart inexplicably beeped like an overwrought R2 unit in his presence. She turned away. "You do make things distressing at times."

"Indubitably, I do. But perhaps you might leave off behaving as if I were Jabba the Hutt. You must acknowledge that betimes, in certain conditions, you do not consider me a loathsome laser brain."

It seemed pure folly to acknowledge this statement, so the princess rubbed her aggrieved hand. Perhaps one pleasant consequence of the explosion of her planet might be that her mother, who interfered dreadfully with her daughter's life, would never observe Leia participating in the manual repair of a space carriage or exchanging pleasantries with a base marauder like Han Solo.

At length, she deigned to reply, "On certain occasions, when you take the opportunity to set aside your scoundrel ways, it may be that your character does not approximate that of a conduit worm."

The uncouth rake laughed at her astute observation, displaying for all the galaxy his low-born manners. "Scoundrel? Scoundrel? Such a word, directed as it is at my person, is eminently pleasing to my ears."

In a complete disregard for propriety, Mr. Solo took Leia's hand and caressed it familiarly. Only he could be so bold!

"Desist your caress, sir!"

"I have no idea to what you are referring."

Leia had been reared properly in the court of Alderaan. Certainly, on occasion, she might have opportunity to encounter the stray military regiment of Stormtroopers, or be obliged to make a swift escape from doom during her missions of diplomatic mercy. However, until today, she had never suffered trepidation and blushes such as she presently endured.

"Cease, I pray, for my hands are soiled with the common grease of drudgery."

The half-witted scalawag made no efforts to halt his untoward stroking of her shockingly naked palm. "No apologies are necessary, Worshipfulness, for, you see, my very own hands are similarly besmirched. What apprehension creases your porcelain brow?"

"Apprehension?"

Mr. Solo abandoned all delicacy and drew the princess toward him. "What a pity it is that you tremble so."

"I must disagree. I am not trembling."

"Your protestations notwithstanding, you have a great opinion of me because I am a scoundrel. Indeed, I have often considered that an increase in the number of scoundrels in your acquaintance would improve your disposition."

"I cannot oblige your misapprehension. I enjoy the company of pleasant Rebel gentlemen."

"I am a pleasant gentleman."

"Not at all. You—"

Without further ado, the reprobate placed his lips upon hers! This gratuitous display of libidinous passion was interrupted by the metallic manservant, C-3PO.

"Sir!" spoke the machine excitedly. "Upon attempting repairs to the equipage, I came upon the reverse power flux coupling and rendered it isolated."

Mr. Solo ceased his ministrations upon the stricken princess and muttered, "How very fortunate a turn of events, Goldenrod. I am in your debt."

"I took no trouble at all about the matter," replied the hapless droid.

Leia slipped away, lest her reputation be as soiled as her hands.

DID YOU KNOW?

Despite repeated efforts, Jane Austen did not see *Northanger Abbey*—originally called *Susan*—published in her lifetime. Henry had negotiated with the publisher Crosby for the manuscript's return in 1816—thirteen years after it had been purchased and then not published. (Only after he had possession of the manuscript, repurchased for the original selling price of £10, did Henry reveal that the author was the same as she who had written *Pride and Prejudice*. Ha!)

Once the manuscript of *Susan* was back in her hands, Austen went through it, changing the heroine's name to Catherine. In 1816 she wrote the "Advertisement by the Authoress" in which she says the book was finished in 1803 and that, since then, "places, manners, books, and opinions have undergone considerable changes." She takes three sentences (out of five) to criticize Crosby—though not by name—for his nonaction: "That any bookseller should think it worth-while to purchase what he did not think it worth-while to publish seems extraordinary." Obviously, the business still irritated her.

In March of 1817 she wrote to her niece Fanny: "Miss Catherine is put upon the Shelve for the present, and I do not know that she will ever come out;—but I have a something ready for Publication, which may perhaps appear about a twelvemonth hence." That something was *The Elliots*; that is, *Persuasion*. But four months after writing this letter Jane Austen was dead, and it was up to others to see that these two novels got published. As her nephew writes, speaking of the continued lives of his aunt's characters as she used to playfully reveal them, "Of the good people in 'Northanger Abbey' and 'Persuasion' we know nothing more than what is written: for before those works were published their author had been taken away from us, and all such amusing communications had ceased forever."

Henry and Cassandra decided on the titles *Northanger Abbey* and *Persuasion* for the two novels, and Henry negotiated a deal with Jane's previous publisher, John Murray. *Northanger Abbey* and *Persuasion* were published together in December of 1817, although the title page says 1818, and 1,750 copies were printed. Included with the novels were the "Advertisement" and a "Biographical Notice of the Author" written by Henry, which was the first effort to make public the details of Jane Austen's life. It is a somewhat idealized portrait, emphasizing Jane's sweetness of temper, Christian faith and virtue, and genius. Henry describes his sister's appearance, accomplishments, wit, and literary taste. According to Henry, "So much did she shrink from notoriety, that no accumulation of fame would have induced her, had she lived, to affix her name to any productions of her pen." What on earth would Jane Austen think of the fame her name has accumulated in the almost two centuries that have passed since her beloved brother wrote that sentence?

Two-Time and Twilight
HEATHER SPIVA

It is a truth, that a legend, a mere trifle of the imagination, must be only that which we assume it to be. However, this business, one of vampires and people, mixing in a way not fashionable or agreeable in the least, is a story recognized for its oddity and charm, one well revealed through the fashion of folklore and fantasy and one duly noted in the simple life of a simple girl.

Bella, a girl of seven and ten, amiable and honest as most girls of her class and status, in want of a future not yet revealed, decides upon Forks as a town of consequence, through circumstances and results of familial decisions both unwanted and dissatisfactory: divorced parents.

Being of a youthful mind, Bella transits with ease, interspersed among individuals her own age and description; an honorable and due position for a girl in need of an esteem-able new life. Bella, once at the first day of her latest endeavors, having made the acquaintance of students, many of whom thought her new and pleasant, had yet to meet one more boy, one not quite so ordinary, by which she could measure her level of acceptance and even, perchance, one of mutual interest.

He sat next to her, this person of similar age and status, who called himself Edward. But this simple glance, a chance meeting of the eyes, was fleeting and much to her dismay, distant. Though he seemed pleasant and easy, seemingly unaffected was he to her greeting. Away he turned as if she reeked of something intolerable to those around her. But his lack of charm wasn't without reason.

This Edward Cullen, hiding amidst the realms of average stature and regular attendance, owned an overwhelmed status. One far superior than Bella assessed! He, smitten not only with her looks and gesture, but by her mere admittance had found his future through her.

"Pray, sir, I am new here," Bella implied with the heartfelt gaze amidst the books and beakers. But with an outreach of her delicate hand, and the scent of her perfected nature, the folly within Edward found an outlet. Had Bella understood the predicament he owned—one horrendous and offensive to her delicate being—she would have agreed with his display of unkempt obscurity and laughed at the rebuff by the imperious youth.

Yet, she understood this not and with a swagger to his look, and the wave of a hand over his coiffed hair, he displaced himself to alleviate himself if not physically, then mentally, away. He could not avail himself to receive her scent!

Bella, perplexed at the man's refusal to speak and being so reasonable a girl, innocent and amiable to be sure, remains in her place now without any cordial feelings toward the uncouth gentleman. If he not be a man of amiable kindness, if he prefers a false dignity, one so uncordial and presumptuous to think she below his level of intelligence, then she need not waste her time accruing that which is merely acquired in vain. She let him be.

But the days progress and a kindness—one not formerly understood or seen by Bella—comes forth through the very Edward who once thought her presence intolerable. Her collective behavior charms the man and beast, and affection she thought not present, emitted itself as a sun on a bright day.

It also, unsatisfactorily, charms the affections of another unusual being; one just as legendary of a creature, a wolf of extraordinary abilities. Bella, much to her dismay at the affections, fancy, and willingness of both men to seek her admiration, begins a journey to choose betwixt them; overwhelmed that she'd received the affections from two unusual beings who seek her fancy!

Both beasts, entirely ignorant of her precarious situation (youthful infatuation and immaturity), seek for what they find; someone for each his own setting and scene; one fit to take as their bride. Bella, being of mind to find both men handsome, brilliant, and indifferent to the conflicting nature of their beings—beings that claim to call themselves boys yet filled with the aura of fantasy—begins a journey; one so mountainous and thrilling that her choice and admiration for both sides begins to stake at her heart, piece by piece.

Most earnestly does Bella sense the urgency for which Edward and Jacob long for her. To where Bella, an esteemed and winsome girl, one so delightful and fair in nature, having found herself the selected choice of both men, is forced to make a decision, one so large in nature, so encompassing in emotional intensity, that the only words available to describe the predicament she duly finds herself availed to are: "Camp Edward or Camp Jacob?"

Did You Know?

Jane Austen is usually called a nineteenth-century writer, and with good reason: Her novels were either written or revised—and they were all first published—in that century. But most of her life (twenty-five of forty-one years) was lived in the prior century, and the events and literature of that time are so influential in her work that we might be justified in calling her an eighteenth-century writer as well. So what was the last quarter of that century in England like? The world of Austen's youth witnessed two of the most significant events in history: the American and French revolutions The names of these events should be capitalized, beginning in, of course, 1775 and 1789. England, we might note, managed to avoid a revolution of its own, but it felt the effects of the revolutionary tide: There were riots and other expressions of discontent with the status quo and of sympathy with the radical sentiments.

∽ Tatooine Abby ∽
VICTORIA SANDBROOK

No one who had ever seen Luke in his infancy would have supposed him born to be a Jedi. His situation in life, the character of his guardians—his aunt and uncle—his own person and disposition, were all equally against him. His uncle was a moisture farmer on Tatooine, without being neglected or poor, and a very respectable man, though his name was Owen Lars—and he had never been handsome. He had a considerable future planned for his enterprise—and fully intended to leave the farm in his nephew's capable hands. Luke's Aunt Beru was a woman of useful plain sense, with a good temper, and, what is more remarkable, with a good constitution. She worked the farm alongside her husband—adopted baby or no; and instead of hating her desert homeland, as anybody might expect, she thrived there and hoped never to leave, watching her nephew grow to excellent health.

A farm family with a boy to help will be always called a fine family, so long as the boy has the arms and legs; but Luke had little else to offer, for he was in general very bored, and for many years of his life, as desperate to leave home as any. He had a thin figure, a sallow skin without colour, sandy, tousled hair, and strong features—so much for his person; and not less unpropitious for Jediism seemed his mind. He was fond of all boys' plays and greatly preferred piloting anything fast not merely to farm work, but to the more heroic enjoyments of childhood like repairing a droid or tending to the household chores. Indeed he had no taste for moisture farming; and if he gathered moisture at all, it was chiefly for the pleasure of adventure—at least so it was conjectured from his always preferring not to do his uncle's bidding. Such were his propensities—his abilities, however, were quite more extraordinary.

At the tender age of six, Luke discovered the location of a lost tool by using the Force. His uncle scolded him thoroughly—not realizing the child knew of the screwdriver thanks to his mental and genetic propensities, only assuming the boy must have hid the tool himself. It did not take another mistake for young Luke to understand that the Force—though he did not know it by name—was not to be trifled with. Four years later, his skill was tested again. After getting lost in a sandstorm with a friend whose actual existence is questionable to this day, Luke slayed a krayt dragon by instinctively throwing a gaffi stick at his throat.

What a strange, unaccountable character!—for with all these symptoms of Jedi at ten years old, he had not a bad heart but a bad temper, was often stubborn and quarrelsome with his uncle, with many interruptions of tyranny. He was moreover wild, hated confinement and cleanliness, and loved nothing so well in the world as speeding through Beggar's Canyon in his landspeeder.

Such was Luke Skywalker at ten. At eighteen, his adventurous spirit was blossoming; he dreamed more often of the stars; his desire to leave Tatooine burgeoned. His love of his family gave way to an inclination for quests, and he grew cunning as he grew older; he had now the pleasure of sometimes believing he could escape the desert for grander worlds. "You'll get your chance to get off this rock" were words that caught his ears now and then; and how welcome were the sounds! To be almost old enough to attend the Flight Academy was an acquisition of higher delight to a boy, whose future had been looking plain as dust the first eighteen years of his life, than a Jedi Padawan trained from birth can ever receive.

DID YOU KNOW?

Jane Austen was buried in Winchester Cathedral on July 24, 1817. The inscription on her tomb speaks of "the benevolence of her heart, the sweetness of her temper, and the extraordinary endowments of her mind" and of her "charity, devotion, faith and purity," but makes no mention of her being an author. In 1872, an additional plaque was placed in the cathedral, and that one does mention her writing. In the 1850s people would come to Winchester Cathedral on pilgrimages to Austen's grave. She was still so little known at that time, her nephew tells us, that the verger (the sacristan and caretaker) didn't know why they were interested and asked if "there was anything particular about that lady." Knowledge of "that lady" and the brilliant, unforgettable ladies and gentlemen she created has certainly spread since then. Jane Austen is surely, and deservedly, the world's favorite novelist.

INDEX

A

D

E

H

I

J

K

L

ABOUT THE AUTHORS

PETER ARCHER is an editor at Adams Media and author of *The Quotable Intellectual* and *I Watch, Therefore I Am*. In his life he has been a college instructor, a convenience-store clerk, and a short-order cook, as well as a lifelong fan of Jane Austen. He lives in Wareham, MA.

JENNIFER LAWLER is a writer and editor and the author or coauthor of more than thirty books. Love of Jane Austen may have convinced her to earn a PhD in English Literature, but it was the love of laughter that made her beg to help create *Bad Austen*.